Meeting the New Demand for Standards

Jonathan R. Warren, *Editor*

NEW DIRECTIONS FOR HIGHER EDUCATION
MARTIN KRAMER, *Editor-in-Chief*

Number 43, September 1983

Paperback sourcebooks in
The Jossey-Bass Higher Education Series

Jossey-Bass Inc., Publishers
San Francisco • Washington • London

Jonathan R. Warren (Ed.).
Meeting the New Demand for Standards.
New Directions for Higher Education, no. 43.
Volume XI, number 3.
San Francisco: Jossey-Bass, 1983.

New Directions for Higher Education Series
Martin Kramer, *Editor-in-Chief*

Copyright © 1983 by Jossey-Bass Inc., Publishers
and
Jossey-Bass Limited

Copyright under International, Pan American, and Universal
Copyright Conventions. All rights reserved. No part of
this issue may be reproduced in any form—except for brief
quotation (not to exceed 500 words) in a review or professional
work—without permission in writing from the publishers.

New Directions for Higher Education (publication number USPS
990-880) is published quarterly by Jossey-Bass Inc., Publishers.
New Directions is numbered sequentially—please order extra
copies by sequential number. The volume and issue numbers
above are included for the convenience of libraries. Second-class
postage rates paid at San Francisco, California, and at
additional mailing offices.

Correspondence:
Subscriptions, single-issue orders, change of address notices, undelivered
copies, and other correspondence should be sent to Subscriptions,
Jossey-Bass Inc., Publishers, 433 California Street, San Francisco
California 94104.

Editorial correspondence should be sent to the Consulting Editor,
Martin Kramer, 2807 Shasta Road, Berkeley, California 94708.

Library of Congress Catalogue Card Number LC 82-84188
International Standard Serial Number ISSN 0271-0560
International Standard Book Number ISBN 87589-953-6

Cover art by Willi Baum
Manufactured in the United States of America

Ordering Information

The paperback sourcebooks listed below are published quarterly and can be ordered either by subscription or as single copies.

Subscriptions cost $35.00 per year for institutions, agencies, and libraries. Individuals can subscribe at the special rate of $21.00 per year *if payment is by personal check.* (Note that the full rate of $35.00 applies if payment is by institutional check, even if the subscription is designated for an individual.) Standing orders are accepted.

Single copies are available at $7.95 when payment accompanies order, and *all single-copy orders under $25.00 must include payment.* (California, Washington, D.C., New Jersey, and New York residents please include appropriate sales tax.) For billed orders, cost per copy is $7.95 plus postage and handling. (Prices subject to change without notice.)

To ensure correct and prompt delivery, all orders must give either the *name of an individual* or an *official purchase order number.* Please submit your order as follows:

Subscriptions: specify series and subscription year.
Single Copies: specify sourcebook code and issue number (such as, HE8).

Mail orders for United States and Possessions, Latin America, Canada, Japan, Australia, and New Zealand to:
Jossey-Bass Inc., Publishers
433 California Street
San Francisco, California 94104

Mail orders for all other parts of the world to:
Jossey-Bass Limited
28 Banner Street
London EC1Y 8QE

New Directions for Higher Education Series
Martin Kramer, *Editor-in-Chief*

HE1 *Facilitating Faculty Development,* Mervin Freedman
HE2 *Strategies for Budgeting,* George Kaludis
HE3 *Services for Students,* Joseph Katz
HE4 *Evaluating Learning and Teaching,* C. Robert Pace
HE5 *Encountering the Unionized University,* Jack H. Schuster
HE6 *Implementing Field Experience Education,* John Duley
HE7 *Avoiding Conflict in Faculty Personnel Practices,* Richard Peairs
HE8 *Improving Statewide Planning,* James L. Wattenbarger, Louis W. Bender
HE9 *Planning the Future of the Undergraduate College,* Donald G. Trites
HE10 *Individualizing Education by Learning Contracts,* Neal R. Berte
HE11 *Meeting Women's New Educational Needs,* Clare Rose
HE12 *Strategies for Significant Survival,* Clifford T. Stewart, Thomas R. Harvey
HE13 *Promoting Consumer Protection for Students,* Joan S. Stark

HE14 *Expanding Recurrent and Nonformal Education,* David Harman
HE15 *A Comprehensive Approach to Institutional Development,* William Bergquist, William Shoemaker
HE16 *Improving Educational Outcomes,* Oscar Lenning
HE17 *Renewing and Evaluating Teaching,* John A. Centra
HE18 *Redefining Service, Research, and Teaching,* Warren Bryan Martin
HE19 *Managing Turbulence and Change,* John D. Millett
HE20 *Increasing Basic Skills by Developmental Studies,* John E. Roueche
HE21 *Marketing Higher Education,* David W. Barton, Jr.
HE22 *Developing and Evaluating Administrative Leadership,* Charles F. Fisher
HE23 *Admitting and Assisting Students after* Bakke, Alexander W. Astin, Bruce Fuller, Kenneth C. Green
HE24 *Institutional Renewal Through the Improvement of Teaching,* Jerry G. Gaff
HE25 *Assuring Access for the Handicapped,* Martha Ross Redden
HE26 *Assessing Financial Health,* Carol Frances, Sharon L. Coldren
HE27 *Building Bridges to the Public,* Louis T. Benezet, Frances W. Magnusson
HE28 *Preparing for the New Decade,* Larry W. Jones, Franz A. Nowotny
HE29 *Educating Learners of All Ages,* Elinor Greenberg, Kathleen M. O'Donnell, William Bergquist
HE30 *Managing Facilities More Effectively,* Harvey H. Kaiser
HE31 *Rethinking College Responsibilities for Values,* Mary Louise McBee
HE32 *Resolving Conflict in Higher Education,* Jane E. McCarthy
HE33 *Professional Ethics in University Administration,* Ronald H. Stein, M. Carlota Baca
HE34 *New Approaches to Energy Conservation,* Sidney G. Tickton
HE35 *Management Science Applications to Academic Administration,* James A. Wilson
HE36 *Academic Leaders as Managers,* Robert H. Atwell, Madeleine F. Green
HE37 *Designing Academic Program Reviews,* Richard F. Wilson
HE38 *Successful Responses to Financial Difficulties,* Carol Frances
HE39 *Priorities for Academic Libraries,* Thomas J. Galvin, Beverly P. Lynch
HE40 *Meeting Student Aid Needs in a Period of Retrenchment,* Martin Kramer
HE41 *Issues in Faculty Personnel Policies,* Jon W. Fuller
HE42 *Management Techniques for Small and Specialized Institutions,* Andrew J. Falender, John C. Merson

Contents

Editor's Notes 1
Jonathan R. Warren

Chapter 1. Accreditation 9
Richard M. Millard
Effective use of accreditation as it continues to evolve is important to maintain educational quality.

Chapter 2. State Concerns for Learning: Quality and State Policy 29
Jeanine Stevens, Bruce D. Hamlett
State agencies conduct an external review of educational quality as indicated by resource allocations, access, consumer protection, and productivity.

Chapter 3. The Major Seventh: Standards as a Leading Tone in Higher Education 39
Clifford Adelman
Too many institutions are not maintaining standards of time, content, expectations, cooperation, and ethical behavior.

Chapter 4. Quality in the Classroom 55
Jonathan R. Warren
If course examinations are developed collaboratively, they can provide the needed information on education achievement.

Chapter 5. Examinations and Quality Control 69
Joseph P. O'Neill
The best way to improve the integrity of our educational standards is by comprehensive examinations that separate teaching from certification of achievement.

Chapter 6. The Administrator's Role in Providing Excellence 81
Thomas J. Hegarty

Chapter 7. What Can Administrators Learn from this Sourcebook? 93
Frederic M. Hudson

Index 99

Editor's Notes

Quality—or the absence of quality—is widely believed to be the most critical educational issue of the current decade. The recent report of the National Commission on Excellence in Education (1983) became a rallying point for the general public, which was already worried about high school and even college graduates whose reading, writing, and computational skills were at embarrassing lows. The report's title, "A Nation at Risk," and its ringing phrases—"the educational foundations of our society are presently being eroded by a rising tide of mediocrity that threatens our very future as a Nation and a people" (National Committee on Excellence, 1983, p. 5)—were in tune with existing fears of economic, social, and technological deterioration. If the report had appeared during a time of comparatively full employment, social problems that seemed manageable, and national self-assurance, it might have had little impact.

The primary reason for the commission's resounding call to rebuild our educational system to its former levels of excellence was a fifteen-year decline in the academic abilities of new high school graduates entering college. That decline, confirmed by a variety of independent sources, has caused commitments of college resources to remedial education to increase, and it has placed a heavier burden on colleges and universities to maintain past levels of academic proficiency among graduates. Nothing else in the report touched on higher education.

A different national commission, the National Commission on Higher Education Issues (1982) was concerned wholly with higher education. While the commission found that higher education had on the whole maintained its quality, there were signs that standards were being jeopardized. The signs included the lower levels of preparation among entering students and the higher average grades that they received in the absence of evidence that they had learned as much as the better-prepared students of earlier years. Together, these observations led to the suspicion that college degrees no longer certify that "those who earn them are men and women of learning" (National Commission on Higher Education Issues, 1982, p. v). When could that certification have been made with assurance?

Others have decried the present quality of higher education, basing their criticisms on two points. First, students are less capable than they used to be, at least in terms of average scores on college admission tests and on English and mathematics placement tests. Second, curricula are less rigorous. This may be true for parts of the curricula in view of the students' poorer preparation. Yet evidence that colleges and universities are less effective now than they have been in the past in turning out well-educated graduates cannot be found—only in part because we lack information about the qualities of the graduates of former years.

The clearest available evidence of the current quality of higher education, to be described more fully in Chapter Four, shows that college graduates are better educated in some respects than they were five, ten, or fifteen years ago, less well educated in other respects, and about the same in still other ways. If that is the case, why has the concern for educational quality in the public schools, which is clearly justified, been extended to higher education? What led Harold Enarson (1983, p. 30) to say that quality in higher education is now in jeopardy, that "shoddiness surrounds us"? Why did George Bonham (1982, p. 109) write of qualitative erosion in higher education and even of "a pattern of sheer incompetence"? Why did staff of the National Commission on Higher Education Issues state in a background paper (American Council on Education, 1981, p. 1) that quality in higher education is "simply a morass?"; indeed, "most analysts and observers agree that quality noticeably declined in the past two decades."

A combination of influences can be found behind the laments for lost quality. It cannot be denied that the deluge of poorly prepared students in the past fifteen years placed a burden on faculty members, who had to restructure their courses to accommodate students who read slowly and poorly, who lack the prior learning that faculty members counted on, and who required the pace of learning to be slowed. Growth in enrollment had permitted newly hired faculty to pick up much of the burden of the poorly prepared students, which left the senior faculty to the more satisfying upper-division and graduate courses. When that growth ended, it limited faculty options. The lag of faculty salaries behind the cost of living increased the frustrations of faculty members, who were already feeling constrained in their choice of teaching assignments. Increasingly tighter budgets exacerbated problems of staffing and facilities. In such circumstances, it is not surprising that the complaints have become claims that quality has been abandoned.

Recognizing both the legitimacy of the public's desire for open access to higher education and the practical consequences of financial constraints and the end of enrollment increases, staff of the National Commission on Higher Education Issues sidestepped the issue of quality to focus on integrity. Institutions, they wrote (American Council on Education, 1981, p. 8-9), should be honest to themselves and their students, offering programs that they are equipped to provide effectively and, in which they maintain standards that are "internally strenuous and externally justifiable.... We could, however, make progress by insisting that whatever education is attempted be undertaken for well-thought-out reasons and in conformity with carefully developed standards that are regularly reexamined, that it be related to available and prospective resources, and that it be done well." Who could object? Yet, these new requirements for making progress are little different from the accreditation standards of twenty or thirty years ago. Those standards have been challenged as inadequate, and accrediting agencies are working hard to replace them. The new requirements avoid coming to grips with quality.

Bonham (1982) echoed this Commission staff position in citing reduced financial resources and poorly prepared students as causes of the recent surge of interest in quality in higher education. The collision between demands for equal access to higher education regardless of prior preparation and competing demands that academic standards should be maintained has torn the educational community, with the exception, as Kerr (1982) noted, of the research universities. While Bonham is ready to acknowledge that declining educational quality is a fact, he despairs of being able to quantify that decline.

Enarson (1983) repeated Bonham's scorn for quantification and even called quality indefinable. He dismissed the concept of value added in education and the comparison of outputs with inputs as "bush-league economics... [and] zeal for qualitification carried to its inherent and logical absurdity" (Enarson, 1983, p. 8). Quality, though indefinable, could be assessed by "individual judgment, the power of informed and thoughtful minds, observation drawing from experience." (Enarson, 1983, p. 8). Arguing that quality in higher education is in jeopardy, Enarson cited the proliferation of courses (8,000 at Ohio State University) and doctoral programs that feed new Ph.D.s into fields that are already saturated.

In Enarson's view, quality could be improved by simplifying the curriculum and by requiring a core of common courses. That is another issue around which conflict swirls. Commenting on the drive for educational excellence, Finn (1983) pointed out that the tightening of educational standards requires attention not only to the level of learning but to the content as well. Specifying the content to be taught has created a schism in higher education between those like Enarson who advocate a single set of core courses that every student takes and those who hold that the diversity among students requires flexible curricula. The concern for quality cannot be addressed effectively until educational pruposes are clear. According to Finn, we must first ask, quality with respect to what?

Accrediting agencies have left the answer to the individual institution, requiring only that the institution answer the question clearly for itself. Then, determination of quality proceeds. In that determination, accrediting associations have pressed institutions to go beyond what Millard calls in Chapter One *definitional-prescriptive standards,* which imitate the characteristics of the institutions that are "good" in the sense that they enjoy high prestige and command the respect of faculty members, administrators, and the general public. These standards have been referred to as *inputs,* or, if they reflect curricular structures or aspects of instruction, *process variables.* They do not assess the consequences of the educational process, students' learning, which some call *outputs.*

Despite the efforts of accrediting agencies to base judgments of quality on the degree to which educational purposes are being accomplished — that is, on evidence of students' learning — success has been elusive. Kirkwood (1981),

p. 65) has pointed out that "assessing outcomes has not been tried and found difficult; rather it has been found difficult and seldom tried." Quality has been equated with the practices of highly regarded institutions by default, and it has been assessed by the informed but impressionistic judgments of knowledgeable experts. Those two elements provide a substantial basis for determinations of quality, but the accrediting agencies have recognized that they lack an anchor and consequently tend to drift. Quality has not yet been tied down.

If higher education is in trouble, as the views of the commissions and individual observers just cited clearly imply, it cannot be because quality has deteriorated except as quality is determined by the characteristics of entering students. That is the only clear support for the claim that quality has dropped. But, any unassailable definition of educational quality must rest to a large extent if not entirely on how close the students come to accomplishing their and the institution's objectives. No author has presented evidence that today's colleges and universities provide educational programs either inferior or superior to those of the recent or distant past.

Individual faculty members may know from personal experience that their own students today are more or less well prepared or committed to study than students of past years, that they perform better or more poorly on equivalent tasks, that they learn more quickly and press for more advanced understanding or that they are slower and progress less far than students in earlier classes. More pertinently, individual faculty members may know that their current courses are better sturctured and better presented and that they produce better results with students than their earlier courses did or that some of their courses have become stale and less effective than past courses but that they have not been refurbished for any of a number of reasons. These observations would constitute direct evidence of a change in educational quality. Yet none of this information, which in principle can be gathered and summarized, is available. This is not to suggest that faculty members should be polled for their opinions but to show just how limited our information is.

We can count the numbers of courses offered, we can observe their diversity, we can form judgments about their academic defensibility, and we can infer that quality is declining. Yet that inference does not rest on information about the kinds of learning that students take from their educational experiences — the well-prepared students in rigorous programs as well as the students who struggle in courses that many faculty members consider undemanding. We can count the number of entering students in remedial courses, we can observe the differences in depth, coverage, and standards between the remedial courses and the regular freshman courses, and we can infer that standards have been abandoned. Yet that inference does not rest on information about the accomplishments of the students who complete the remedial courses and move on to more acceptable kinds of study or of the students who enter college as well prepared as students of prior years. Most faculty members would no doubt prefer better-prepared students, smaller classes, and better pay, and all three aspects of college teaching have probably deteriorated in recent years. Yet nothing in those observations allows us unequivocally to infer that higher education today is better or worse than it was in past years or that it is better or worse than it might be in a society that valued education above all else and that was unstinting in its allocation of resources to education. Judgments about the quality of American higher education are based on little more than folklore, nostalgic reminiscences, and personal preferences.

Can this be changed? Should it be changed? Enarson (1983) thinks it cannot and is not concerned about it. Kirkwood (1981) thinks that it can and should but that it is difficult. Astin (1979) and Solmon (1981) think that it can and should and that it would not be unreasonably difficult. The last two authors advocate use of multiple indicators of student learning. Any one indicator is limited, but collectively they would permit defensible inferences about the quality of education.

Certainly, educational quality can be defined, although no simple definition will suffice. Even the purposes of complex, multipurpose institutions can be defined in terms of the collective purposes of their divisions and departments. And, even when the formal purposes contain more jargon than they do information, courses in a department are organized and integrated to bring students to some set of describable educational accomplishments. Faculty members know from direct experience with students and students' papers, examinations, and other products when a class has been unusually successful, unusually limited, or comparable in accomplishment to most prior classes. Thus a rise or fall in educational quality within an institution should be reflected as a systematic rise or fall in faculty members' perceptions of student accomplishment. Faculty members could describe the specific accomplishments of their classes, and those descriptions could be organized into a systematic, detailed, collective statement of the accomplishments of the students during the preceding term. Knowledgeable persons could compare collective statements of accomplishment from several institutions. If the institutions were similar in their purposes but differed appreciably in their accomplishments, these persons could make defensible judgments about the relative quality of those institutions.

The information these steps would produce might be quantitative, and therefore might not be respected by Bonham (1982), Enarson (1983), and others. Probably some information would be quantitative and some qualitative. Both kinds of information are useful. Baseball players are described quantitatively in terms of batting averages and other statistics, but they are also judged qualitatively—for their ability to field their position, to make the big play, to spark a rally. Quantitative indicators of educational quality are straw men for those who object to them in principle. At times, quantitative indicators are almost worthless; at other times, they are the most valuable kind of information available. Useful information on educational quality can only originate from events or occurrences that can be described clearly enough that someone who was not present when they happened can understand them. Summarizing that information may require a narrative description or a table of figures. Any complex or extensive body of information is likely to require both qualitative and quantitative description.

In summary, the cries of alarm that are being heard about quality in higher education rest on clear but limited evidence—poorly prepared entering students—that is not supported by other clear but limited evidence—achievement test scores of graduates. A portent more serious for higher education than poor preparation among entering students is our lack of clear and direct evidence about what higher education is accomplishing with students. While questions of quality are necessarily complex and multifaceted, involving administrators, faculty, curricular structure, student preparation and commitment, fiscal soundness, physical facilities, and other components of higher education, one central element must be the students' academic accomplishments. Information about that central element is disturbingly scarce.

Jonathan R. Warren
Editor

References

American Council on Education. "Quality in American Higher Education." Unpublished background paper for the National Commission on Higher Education Issues, Washington, D.C.: American Council on Education, 1981.

Astin, A. W. "Student-Oriented Management: A Proposal for Change." In *Evaluating Educational Quality: A Conference Summary.* Washington, D.C.: Council on Postsecondary Accreditation, 1979.

Bonham, G. W. "Measuring Indicators of Quality." In E. Kuhns and S. V. Martorana (Eds.), *Qualitative Methods for Institutional Research.* New Directions for Institutional Research, no. 34. San Francisco: Jossey-Bass, 1982.

Enarson, H. L. "Quality—Indefinable but Not Unattainable." *Educational Record,* 1983, *64* (1), 7-9.

Finn, C. E. "The Drive for Educational Excellence: Moving Toward a Public Consensus." *Change,* 1983, *15* (3), 14-22.

Kerr, C. "The Uses of the University Two Decades Later: Postscript 1982." *Change,* 1982, *14* (7), 23-31.

Kirkwood, R. "Process or Outcomes—A False Dichotomy." In T. M. Stauffer (Ed.), *Quality—Higher Education's Principal Challenge.* Washington, D.C.: American Council on Education, 1981.

National Commission on Excellence in Education. *A Nation at Risk: The Imperative for Educational Reform.* Washington, D.C.: U.S. Department of Education, 1983.

National Commission on Higher Education Issues. *To Strengthen Quality in Higher Education.* Washington, D.C.: American Council on Education, 1982.

Solmon, L. C. "A Multidimensional Approach to Quality." In T. M. Stauffer (Ed.), *Quality—Higher Education's Principal Challenge.* Washington, D.C.: American Council on Education, 1981.

Jonathan R. Warren conducts research on undergraduate curricula and student learning at Educational Testing Service's Berkeley office.

How accreditation developed its characteristics, use of standards, and conception of quality.

Accreditation

Richard M. Millard

Accreditation does not determine institutional or program quality. Educational quality is a characteristic of institutions or programs, not of accrediting associations. The primary responsibility for institutional and program integrity and quality assurance rests with the individual programs, institutions, or governance systems in higher education. The commitment to educationally sound objectives and effective means of attaining them lies with faculties, administrators, trustees, students, and alumni of programs, institutions, or systems. While accreditation cannot create quality, it has or it should have a crucial role in determining whether an institution or program has accepted and is carrying out its commitment to quality. It also provides incentives to encourage enhancement of quality.

Accreditation is the primary communal self-regulatory means of academic and educational quality assessment and enhancement. As a condition, it is a status granted to an educational institution or program that has been found by its peers, including professional and public representatives, to meet stated criteria bearing on educational quality and accomplishment. As a process, it has two fundamental purposes: to attest to the quality of an institution or program and to assist in improving that quality. As an activity, accreditation is the members of academic and professional communities working together to develop and validate standards, to assess the adequacy of their own operations, and to offer peer judgment and guidance to assure students and the general public of the integrity and quality of education.

J. R. Warren (Ed.). *Meeting the New Demand for Standards.* New Directions for Higher Education, no. 43. San Francisco: Jossey-Bass, September 1983.

Accreditation attests that an institution or program has clearly defined and educationally appropriate objectives, that it maintains conditions under which it is reasonable to expect that they will be achieved, that it appears to be accomplishing them, and that it can be expected to continue to do so. Accreditation is accomplished through accrediting associations that consist of institutions, programs, professional groups and their representatives, and representatives of the public. The strengths and the weaknesses of accreditation reflect its status as the academic conscience of the education community.

The accreditation process has four major components: The institution or program develops an adequate statement of institutional or program mission, goals, and objectives. The institution or program conducts an effective analytic self-study focused on the way and the extent to which it achieves its objectives. A selected group of peers carries out an on-site visit to evaluate the adequacy and accuracy of the self-study and the institution's effectiveness in meeting its objectives. Finally, an independent accrediting commission reviews the self-study and the report of the site visitors and decides, in view of its standards, whether the institution or program is worthy of accreditation.

Types of Accreditation

There are two types of accreditation and accrediting associations—institutional and specialized or programmatic. Institutional accreditation is carried out by institutional accrediting associations, which are national or regional in scope and which include the institutions that have achieved and maintain accreditation. Institutional accreditation focuses on the institution as a whole. Thus, it gives attention not only to the educational program but to such areas as effective management, student personnel services, financial and physical resources, administrative strength, and consumer protection. In addition to nine regional commissions, four national institutional accrediting associations accredit specialized types of separate institutions, three of which include primarily proprietary schools: the Association of Independent Colleges and Schools (for business schools), the National Association of Trade and Technical Schools), the National Home Study Council (for correspondence schools), and the American Association of Bible Colleges.

Specialized accreditation is carried out by accrediting associations within specific professional, occupational, or disciplinary areas that usually are closely related not only to the educational programs but to the professional associations in these areas. Specialized accrediting associations accredit programs or schools in complex institutions that prepare professionals, technicians, or members of special occupations. Most specialized associations require that the programs evaluated be part of an institutionally accredited college or university. Through their relations with professional associations, they are able to provide not only assurance that the program is educationally sound but that it is relevant to current practice in the appropriate professional field.

Not all disciplines in postsecondary and higher education have specialized or programmatic accrediting bodies. Most disciplines within the arts and sciences are considered integral parts of the institutional core and fall within the purview of institutional accreditation. On the whole, programmatic accreditation is developed in and applies to areas that prepare persons for particular occupational or professional fields and in which there is a recognized first professional degree. These tend to be fields where issues of public welfare, health, safety, and need for assurance of professional competence are matters of academic, professional, and public concern.

Interassociation Activities

Until mid century, accrediting associations, whether institutional or specialized, tended to operate independently. There was little or no systematic communication among them, and there was no oversight of their activities. As early as the 1920s, some institutions had become concerned about the number and impact of specialized accrediting bodies. However, a coordinating agency was not established until 1949 — at the urging of college presidents — by seven of the institutionally based higher education organizations. The National Commission on Accrediting (NCA) was established in an attempt to reduce the number of specialized agencies (twenty-three at the time) and incorporate their activities under the regional associations, although the Western association was just being formed, and it had not started accrediting. NCA did not attain either objective. However, it did establish a review and recognition process that most of the specialized accrediting associations voluntarily subscribed to and applied for. NCA was funded directly by institutions and gained its influence from the commitment of some institutions to invite only NCA-recognized associations onto campus. It helped to establish a bond among the specialized associations and to increase their awareness of one another.

In the same year, the regional commissions established a very different kind of group, the National Committee of Regional Accrediting Agencies (NCRAA), to facilitate cooperation and the development of common or complementary policies among those associations. In 1969, the NCRAA became the Federation of Regional Accrediting Commissions of Higher Education (FRACHE). While federation policy setting required five of the six regional commissions to concur, it opened a continuing forum for testing new ideas, dealing with common concerns, and exchanging information. It had minimal involvement with the NCA or the specialized accrediting associations.

With the increasing prominence of accreditation and with the federal government's use after 1952 of accreditation as a condition of eligibility for federal funds, the need for developing a single coordinating and recognizing body for accrediting associations became insistently clear. The first steps toward a merger between NCA and FRACHE took place in 1971, and after much negotiating the merger occurred in 1975. The Council on Postsecondary

Accreditation (COPA) was the result. COPA has evolved to become an integral part of the self-regulating structure that characterizes accreditation. A voluntary organization of accrediting associations and national postsecondary organizations, it has three primary objectives: to recognize accrediting associations that accredit institutions and programs of postsecondary education on the basis of demonstrated need and specified standards relating to accrediting policies and practices; to provide national leadership and understanding for accreditation by cultivating broad understanding of accreditation, serving as a spokesman for accreditation at the national level, and interacting with educational institutions, government agencies, foundations, and other interested groups on matters of accreditation; and to provide services to accrediting associations, postsecondary educational institutions, and the public by assisting in improving the general accrediting process, improving the policies and practices of recognized accrediting associations, facilitating coordination among accrediting associations, and encouraging, sponsoring, and conducting research relating to the understanding and improvement of accreditation.

Accreditation: Origins and Development

Beginnings of Regional Associations. The regional accrediting associations began in the last decades of the nineteeth century. During this period, higher education represented a disparate composite of institutions. The leading institutions faced three related problems. The first was admissions from secondary schools that varied considerably in character and quality. The second was transfer from institution to institution, particularly from colleges that maintained their own preparatory programs and did not clearly distinguish between preparatory and college-level courses. The third was admission to the newly emerging graduate schools of students from a variety of undergraduate colleges across the country. As a result, the major institutions in various sections of the country formed associations to increase articulation of secondary schools, to deal with problems of transfer and cooperation, and to develop lists of schools whose students could be admitted for graduate study.

The New England Association of Colleges and Secondary Schools began in 1885 as the result of requests from principals and headmasters of academies to President Eliot of Harvard to bring together college leadership and secondary school personnel. The Middle States Association of Colleges and Schools was organized in 1887, followed by the North Central Association of Colleges and Secondary Schools and the Association of Colleges and Secondary Schools of the Southern Association in 1895. The Northwest Association of Schools and Colleges was established in 1917, and the Western College Association was founded in 1924.

None of the regional associations began accreditation of higher education immediately. The first to do so was North Central, which published its first list of accredited institutions in 1913. North Central was followed in 1917 by the Southern Association and in 1919 by the Middle States. Northwest began accrediting in 1923. The Western Association did not begin accrediting until 1948. The New England Association, the first to be organized, utilized criteria for admission from an early date but did not undertake periodic review of institutions until 1952.

Beginnings of Specialized Accreditation. Specialized accreditation antedates regional and institutional accreditation. Specialized accreditation reflects the interest of professional and occupational associations and fields in the adequacy of educational preparation for practice in fields where concern for public health, safety, and welfare and public and professional expectations of professional competence are high. The associations are also concerned with defining or delimiting their professional fields and ensuring that educational requirements are related to current requirements for professional practice.

The American Medical Association, established in 1847, developed a committee on medical education. However, not until it was reorganized around 1900 did this organization turn its attention to strengthening medical education and ensuring that it had a sound scientific base. It published its first differentiated list of medical schools, based on the percentage of licensure examination failures, in 1905. In 1907, the 160 existing schools were classified as approved, on probation, or unapproved. Eighty-two schools appeared on the approved list. With help from the Carnegie Foundation, Abraham Flexner and N. P. Colwell visited all existing medical schools. The result was the Flexner report of 1910, which revolutionized medical education. By 1915, the number of medical schools had dropped to 95 (a 40 percent reduction), and medical education was established on a strong scientific base.

Three other professional associations came into existence and began accrediting activities at about the same time. The American Osteopathic Association was established in 1897 and began accrediting in 1901. The Association of American Law Schools and the Society of American Foresters both began in 1900. By the beginning of World War II, there were at least sixteen other specialized associations that accredited colleges and universities. Today, the Council on Postsecondary Accreditation recognizes thirty-seven specialized accrediting bodies.

Other Early Accreditation Activities. Beginning in 1882, the American Association of University Women inspected and listed institutions that, according to its standards, produced graduates meriting membership in the association. It continued this listing until 1963.

Of considerably more impact was the listing published by the Association of American Universities (AAU). As early as 1904, the University of Berlin had used AAU membership as a basis for admitting graduate students. The German universities requested the AAU to prepare a somewhat longer list of certified institutions. Beginning in 1914, the AAU did so. At the outset, the list was based on records of transfer and graduate students at AAU institutions. However, from 1923 onward, inspection visits to institutions were the basis for inclusion in the list. This practice continued until 1948. Soon after, the Western Association and the New England Association began accrediting in the full sense.

One early attempt that might have given quality assessment in this country a very different history if it had succeeded was carried out by the United States Bureau of Education. In cooperation with the AAU, Kendric Babcock, a bureau specialist, prepared a list that used achievement of advanced degrees to rate undergraduate colleges. President Taft had the list withdrawn, and President Wilson vetoed the idea on the grounds that the federal government had no business assessing higher education institutions. This was the list that the AAU sent to Germany. If Presidents Taft and Wilson had not decided against it, quality assessment in higher education might well have become a function of the federal government.

Evolving Nature of Standards. Interestingly, some of the early standards used by accrediting associations and groups, such as the Bureau of Education and the AAU, were essentially results- or outcome-oriented. For example, AAU institutions used records of transfer and graduate student success. These were essentially student outcome measures. On the whole, however, the earliest standards used by accrediting associations can be described as definitional-prescriptive; that is, they were quantitatively reportable institutional characteristics that defined what a "good" institution was. In most areas, these characteristics were input factors, and the implicit norm was what the "best" institutions did, how the "best" institutions were organized, and what the "best" institutions offered. In a sense, these characteristics were an extension of the elitism that led the faculty of Yale University in 1828 to close the curriculum for all time against intrusions by such deviations from true education as the natural sciences and modern foreign languages. Although the Land Grant Act and Eliot's adoption at Harvard of the elective system based on the German model have intervened, the assumption that quality can be defined by characteristics, including curriculum, drawn from the elite institutions has persisted.

The major break in the definitional-prescriptive approach, led by the North Central Association, came in the 1930s. In 1929, North Central appointed a committee on the revision of standards. The committee report was completed in 1934 and published in 1936 (Zook and Haggerty, 1936). North Central adopted and implemented the report in part. The Middle States Association was the first to implement the report in full. Essentially, the report proposed that an institution should be judged not on the basis of a series of fixed characteristics but in terms of the purposes that it seeks to serve and of the total pattern that it presents as an institution of higher education. This approach might be described as a mission-objective model, with the standards developed as conditions of effective fulfillment of mission. With this model, the concept of accreditation changed from a process primarily of assessment to a process of assessment that provided institutions with external stimulation for continued improvement. Accreditation thereby acquired a dual function: quality assessment and quality enhancement. With this development, the analytic self-study gained new importance, as did the role of the visiting team as a group of peer consultants. Over a relatively short period of time, the mission-objective model was adopted by all the regional associations, and it gained considerable ground with the specialized associations as well. However, the tension between the mission-objective and the definitional-prescriptive models has tended to persist.

A third approach, which tends to characterize many of the specialized accrediting associations, can be described as the program-professional model. It modifies the mission-objective approach in that the mission or objective is not the institution's overall mission or total pattern but rather the institution's mission or objectives in education for a particular professional field, modified by conditions and expectations of practitioners within the field itself. Thus, this model is designed to assure that the program is both educationally sound and relevant to current practice in the field. If offers a unique opportunity for consideration of outcome factors, but that opportunity has not always been recognized or used by the agencies in question. Moreover, the program-professional model can create tensions within an institution between programs, between programs and the institution as a whole, or between institutions and professional associations. This potential led to the effort, which emerged in the 1930s, of some presidents and presidential associations to curb both the proliferation and the independence of specialized accrediting associations. Formation of the National Commission on Accrediting was part of this effort. The same concern motivates the recent charge of the Carnegie Foundation for the Advancement of Teaching (1982) that specialized accreditation constitutes a threat to institutional autonomy and independence. However, this charge tends to overlook the fact that, in developing professional programs, an institution accepts responsibilities for preparation of competent professionals and stakes its integrity on doing so effectively.

The G.I. Bill and Federal Concerns. In 1944, the Congress passed the Servicemen's Opportunity Act, generally known as the G.I. Bill, and thereby brought the federal government into higher education in a major way. As originally passed, the bill had no provision for distinguishing legitimate institutions from unscrupulous ones. The result was a series of scandals. The Congress turned to the self-regulatory structure of the academic community for help in correcting the situation. To be eligible to receive federal funds, institutions would have to meet certain conditions. One condition was that an agency recognized by the Commissioner of Education as a reliable authority on the quality of education or training offered had to accredit the institution. There were alternate ways of establishing eligibility, such as the three-letter rule and direct program approval by the Veterans Administration. However, the three-letter rule required acceptance of transfer credits by three accredited institutions, and the Veterans Administration was encouraged to use accreditation, when it applied, in place of its own review. The commissioner was directed to prepare a list of recognized accrediting agencies. In addition to accreditation, an institution had also to be authorized or licensed to operate in its state. These provisions have been repeated with little or no modification in all subsequent major higher education legislation, including the landmark Higher Education Act of 1965. While making accreditation a condition of eligibility for federal funds did not technically change the voluntary nature of accreditation, it clearly created a major incentive for institutions desiring federal funds to seek accreditation.

Increasing Role of Regional Accreditation. After the AAU list of approved institutions was withdrawn in 1948, institutional accreditation was left to the regional accrediting associations. With accreditation as a condition of eligibility for federal funds, the pressure increased on the regionals to expand their scope. They had accredited primarily nonprofit baccalaureate institutions. They adapted slowly and with some reluctance to the rapidly growing community college movement, but they resisted consideration of proprietary institutions and vocational and technical institutes. The issue of proprietary schools reached a head with a suit in 1969 by Marjorie Webster Junior College, a proprietary junior college in Washington, D.C., against the Middle States Commission on Higher Education, which had refused to consider it because of its proprietary status. While the final decision was in favor of Middle States, it was something of a Pyrrhic victory. Soon after, not only Middle States but other regional associations changed their rules and began to accredit proprietary schools, partially as a reult of the negative publicity that ensued but more fundamentally as a result of growing recognition of the North Central principle that the form of governance, while relevant, is not a determinant of quality.

The occupations-vocational issue took a somewhat different form. The primary pressure to extend accreditation to occupational and technical schools came from the political community, where it was rather clearly related to the issue of eligibility for federal funds. The lead was taken by governors and state legislators, who over a period of four or five years passed a series of resolutions at national and regional meetings requesting the regionals to extend accreditation in these areas. The various regionals responded in different ways. Three developed separate commissions, while three expanded the scope of their existing commissions. Somewhat ironically, by the time the Congress authorized the Commissioner of Education in 1972 to recognize the right of state vocational agencies to attest to the quality of vocational education programs for eligibility for federal funds, all six regionals had provided for accreditation of occupational and vocational schools.

Emergence of National Institutional Accrediting Bodies. Unlike the regional associations, the national institutional accrediting bodies are primarily concerned with particular types of postsecondary institutions. The National Home Study Council began in 1926. The American Association of

Bible Colleges was established in 1947, the Association of Independent Colleges and Schools in 1952, and the National Association of Trade and Technical Schools in 1965. All four operate in areas that the regionals were reluctant to occupy in the 1940s and 1950s. With the possible expection of the National Association of Trade and Technical Schools, these organizations were not developed primarily to provide federal conditions of eligibility for their schools. However, there is little question that passage of the Servicemen's Opportunity Act in 1952 greatly enhanced their position. Regardless of the conditions that gave rise to them or that enhanced their development, they serve a large and important sector of the postsecondary education community.

Expansion of Specialized Accreditation. While the number of specialized accrediting agencies probably has not increased as much as it would have without the National Commission on Accrediting (NCA), the number has increased considerably since 1949. By 1957, NCA recognized twenty-one specialized agencies, all older than NCA itself. By 1965, the number had increased to twenty-nine. In 1983, the Council on Postsecondary Accreditation recognized thirty-seven, a decrease of two since 1975. However, one of this number is the Committee on Allied Health Education and Accreditation, which includes twenty-four collaborating organizations in allied health areas and sixteen joint review committees that review different specialized allied health programs. Thus, the actual number of programs accredited has increased from thirty-three in 1965 to sixty-seven in 1982.

This increase in the numbers of specialized agencies and programs accredited clearly reflects the development of specialty fields, an unavoidable phenomenon as knowledge advances and as new specialties and professional areas emerge. Most of the increase has been in technical areas—the majority in allied health. If proliferation simply means increase in numbers, then clearly there has been proliferation. However, if proliferation means duplication and unwarranted increase, the answer may be quite different. The problem is not one of checking unwanted growth but one of dealing with desirable growth— with the need for educated and trained individuals and with the demands that preparing these individuals place on institutions.

Accreditation in the Period of Expansion. The 1960s and 1970s saw the most rapid expansion of enrollments in higher education in the history of this country. This expansion was the result not only of the post–World War II baby boom but of national policy launched under the Great Society and continued in subsequent administrations. This policy placed the emphasis on education as the door to social mobility.

The period of expansion severely strained the accrediting associations. The number of reviews increased tremendously. By expanding their use of volunteers, the associations were able to meet the challenge. However, the great increase in the number of institutions made it inevitable that some programs, particularly at the graduate level, were not monitored as carefully as they might have been.

To complicate the picture, federal assistance to higher education saw a rapid growth during this period, particularly student assistance in the form of grants and guaranteed student loans. While most institutions handled federal funds with integrity, a few did not. Those cases were blown out of proportion, with charges of fraud, abuse, and error, and the accrediting agencies were blamed for not policing their institutions more effectively. Critics forget that, while accrediting associations can and do attest to the general fiscal integrity of institutions at the time of accreditation, they cannot continuously police specific institutional activities, not is it their function to enforce specific federal regulations. As a result, the tensions between the federal government and accrediting associations began to increase.

The most serious threat to the credibility of higher education and accreditation came from the student unrest of the late 1960s and the early 1970s. While the unrest had its roots in social and international conditions that lay outside the academy, it seriously undermined public confidence in higher education. To many it appeared that something was seriously awry not only in the methods of higher education but in its objectives, structure, and basic assumptions as well.

At the same time, recognition was growing that traditional higher education is by no means the whole of post–high school education. In 1972, Congress took the initiative by declaring in amendments to the Higher Education Act of 1965 that the universe of that measure was postsecondary education, with higher education a subclass within it. On both federal and state levels, this redefinition had the effect of extending concerns and benefits to all legitimate educational opportunities beyond high school. Another development involved the increasing emphasis among governments and the public on protection of students as educational consumers. A number of states developed authorization or licensure laws, and accrediting associations began to appreciate their consumer protection role. Finally, the concept of accountability became far more central, not only in government circles but in the academic community itself. The concept extended both to fiscal integrity and management and to academic results.

As the period of expansion drew to a close in the mid and late seventies, higher education institutions became progressively more involved with off-campus programs. These programs were not limited to the vicinity or even the state of the parent institution; they extended across state, regional, and even national boundaries. Many were programs on military bases. Both off-campus programs in general and military programs in particular pose a series of problems for accrediting associations: reviewing off-campus operations in relation to the institution as a whole, the same criteria are relevant to off-campus sites, finally, the cost of sending visiting teams to a dozen or more sites around the world. With support from the Kellogg Foundation, the Council on Postsecondary Accreditation undertook a major study of accreditation of nontraditional and off-campus education in 1978. One result of the study was establishment of the principle that an institution's integrity is as closely involved with its off-campus operations as it is with its home campus operations and that the same criteria should be applied to off-campus operations and to home campus operations.

Accreditation and Retrenchment. The period of expansion has been succeeded by what can only be described as a period of retrenchment: The number of eighteen- to twenty-four-year-olds has decreased, and the general trend in enrollment is downward. Some institutions will not survive. Others will have a difficult time in maintaining sufficient enrollment. The fiscal stringencies produced by the recent recession and, for public institutions, the decrease in and resulting competition for state funds pose additional problems. Finally, the issue of accountability has become even more acute, heightened as it has been by the need for a clear rationale for the use of the limited funds available. All these factors have tremendously increased the competition among institutions for students and funds. Under such circumstances, the temptation is great for some institutions to try to meet the competition by lowering standards and by adding off-campus programs designed more for market appeal than to provide quality educational services. This creates additional problems not only for institutional accrediting bodies but for specialized accrediting bodies as well.

This period of retrenchment already has led to some closures and mergers. The accrediting community is particularly concerned that students in these circumstances be protected. The retrenchment has also led to further erosion of public confidence in higher education and in the ability of accrediting associations to assess quality and encourage its enhancement when survival is at stake. For these and other reasons, the issue of quality has been identified as one of the most critical issues for higher education in this decade. It is an issue that extends considerably beyond the institutions and the accrediting associations. It has in effect become everybody's business.

As already noted, the accrediting associations have been dealing with quality assessment and quality enhancement for some seventy years. Their approach to these issues has evolved over time. The accrediting associations are constantly reviewing and validating their standards and procedures and adapting to changing conditions. Theoretically, their standards and procedures should be as adaptable to retrenchment as they are to expansion. However, it is critical at this point for the premises and concepts involved to be clearly understood by the academic community and by the various publics that the associations serve.

Quality, Educational Integrity, and Accreditation

The debate about the nature and definition of quality is about as old as the human species itself. It is neither possible nor desirable to recount the history of that debate here, since our concern is with the monitoring of educational quality. However, there is a basic definitional problem caused in part by mixing different but related terms. These terms include *definition, standard, criterion,* and *index.* A definition is a statement of the precise meaning or significance of a word or term — in this case *quality*, particularly as it characterizes education or the educational process. In contrast, a *standard* is a norm or acknowledged measure of the status or condition characterized by quality. A single standard can designate one aspect of the condition and serve as one basis for judgment of approximation to that condition, although a number of standards may be necessary to judge whether the condition in fact is met. *Criterion* and *standard* are often used interchangeably. When both terms are used, *criterion* usually implies a further specification of the standard or a test or rule for assessing whether the standard has been achieved, while an *index* is a sign or indicator that some condition prevails. In far too many discussions about accreditation, standards, criteria, and even indexes are confused with definitions. As a result, the parties to discussion are talking about means of determining the status or partial characteristics of the status, not about the condition itself. To define quality in terms of faculty characteristics, or resources available, or even outcomes is to create such confusion. To judge that accreditation is irrelevant to quality because it relies on input factors is to assume a partial definition in terms of a particular set of criteria or indexes; thus, this judgment may miss the point altogether. Some of the research that concludes rather quickly that there is little correlation between accrediting standards and educational quality may in fact be using an alternate set of indexes to define quality.

If the standards must be relevant to and in some sense derived from the definition of quality, a far more fundamental problem lies in the definition itself. If a definition is to be more than an arbitrary stipulation, part of its relevance or significance lies in what can be done with it and in how it relates to or orders its universe of application.

Definitions of Quality. At least four definitions of quality have been applied in the educational sphere. It is important to look briefly at each definition to assess its relevance to standard setting and to determine how it orders the educational universe. The first definition of quality is that quality is in fact undefinable. It is an ineffable characteristic of something — in this case education — that is recognized intuitively, and something either has it or does not. This is a rather widely held view, even within the academic community. However, it is not very useful.

The second definition approaches quality from the standpoint of social consensus. It usually is refined so that quality becomes what is agreed on by knowledgeable people. It sounds democratic, perhaps because it places quality in the eye of the beholders, but it does not advance us very far beyond the first definition. Even if we limit the consensus to knowledgeable people, such people disagree, and the definition itself gives no basis for deciding among the judgments of knowledgeable groups. The current reliance on statistical surveys to determine what the components of quality should be makes the definition of quality a popularity vote.

The third definition uses a single paradigm to signify quality. This is essentially the Platonic view. If such a paradigm could be used, it would clearly order its universe. Individual objects—in this case, individual educational institutions or programs—would embody the paradigm to varying degrees. Standards in the area could either be derived from it, or they would be norms for assessing approximation to it. The difficulty lies in identifying or discovering the paradigm. In the Platonic universe, quality was to be discovered through dialogue that moved people ever closer to the universal or the ideal. In practice, the third definition has tended to take the form of a single model of what connotes the ideal college or university. Usually, this model has been someone's idea of the best college or the better colleges. Thus, the third definition is closely related to the definitional-prescriptive concept of standards, and it has all the elitism, rigidity, and qualitative criteria that that involves. Where this definition is applied, the result is likely to be homogenization—leading institutions, copies of leading institutions, copies of copies of leading institutions—and disregard for the excellence in institutions or programs of radically differing types.

The fourth definition accepts the idea of a paradigm, but it defines quality contextually, thus placing the paradigm within the activity itself. Quality is thus defined as achievement in kind. The quality of a knife lies in its ability to cut what it is supposed to cut. Quality is clearly related to objective—an objective appropriate to the entity or the process in question. In relation to an educational institution or program, quality is a function of the effectiveness with which the institution or program uses resources to achieve appropriate educational objectives. Thus an institution's or program's norm is implicit within it, and its quality is determined by how well its various components cohere in achieving its educational objective or objectives. Students, faculty, resources, location or locations, and results are integral to the quality of the operation, and the key to integration of all these elements in quality is mission or objective and its educational appropriateness. Thus one can expect quality equally in a complex university, a single-purpose institution, a community college, a selective liberal arts college, an occupational or technical institute, and a center for adult and continuing education.

At first glance, the fourth definition may seem to imply that the standards for assuring quality must be unique to each institution or program. That is not so. As the conditions for assessing effective use of resources for the achievement of educationally appropriate objectives, standards are generalizable. In fact they must be generalizable, given our definition of standard. However, the application of these standards, must be adaptable to many different conditions and situations. What the standards address basically are the components or factors involved in achieving operationally effective educational synthesis in the light of objectives.

Quality in the Educational Context. If we accept achievement in kind as the basic concept of quality and effective use of resources to achieve appropriate educational objectives as its specification in education, we make quality not only contextual but judgmentally determinable and comparable given the context. Further, this concept of quality is applicable to educational activities, students, programs, larger units such as colleges or schools within institutions, institutions as a whole, and even systems.

Obviously students are the focus of and reason for educational activities. But the quality of a student's educational activity has to be determined contextually, and that context includes what students bring with them, their educational objectives, how they use the opportunities or resources available, how their objectives cohere with the program or institutional objectives, what takes place as a result, and the extent to which the objectives are realized. In this framework, value added, outcomes, results, and the processes for attaining them all become relevant to the quality of education participated in and achieved. The results are both unique to individual students and comparable among groups of students who have similar objectives.

This does not assume that students' objectives are fixed at the beginning of their educational experience. Part of a student's objective may be to discover what his or her objectives are — even whether he or she has any. But, as students' objectives become more focused in the process, so do the conditions for achieving them as well as the results or outcomes to be expected. This is not an argument for grading on value-added factors only, for part of the educational process for the individual involves recognizing levels of achievement essential to attainment of objectives. This conception of quality of education as achievement in kind as that achievement relates to the individual student recognizes four things: first, as objectives change, the determination of the quality of the student's educational experiences also change; second, the quality of the student's education is not a function of institutional type or social role stereotypes; third, the quality of the student's experience can vary considerably among students in the same institution or program; fourth, what the institution or program provides are conditions that may be more or less conducive to assurance of that quality.

Obviously, facilitation of students' achievement of their educational objectives is critical on a program level. However, other factors also enter the picture. A program, particularly on a professional, preprofessional, or occupational level, presupposes that students have focused their objectives on that program area. Accordingly, the objectives of the program and their adaptability to student objectives and background become crucial. Clearly defined program objectives are essential, as is spelling out the conditions needed for achieving them and communicating these to students. The objectives include the competencies to be attained and the rationale for attaining them, whether by traditional or by nontraditional means. In occupational and professional or preprofessional areas, where specialized accreditation becomes relevant, determining that these competencies are adequate for practice in the field must involve not only the program faculty and the institution but professionals or practitioners in the field as well. If the objectives are clear, then three questions arise: Are the resources adequate to achieve those objectives? Are the resources used in a way that is conducive to achieving the objectives? Have students who completed the program achieved the objectives? Quite clearly, the types of resources required—facilities, equipment, faculty and faculty qualifications, learning resources, and even research activity—vary with program objectives. Outcomes are most relevant to program objectives, and with such objectives desired outcomes can best be defined in terms of experiential competencies. While the quality of programs within an institution can vary, the institution's integrity and quality are at stake in the effectiveness with which its programs fulfill their specific objectives. This is particularly important when we consider the role of specialized or professional accrediting associations and their relation to the issue of institutional integrity.

On the institutional level, program quality and institutional quality can be one and the same when the institution is relatively small and essentially single-purpose in character. At more complex institutions, particularly in systems involving multiple programs and services that have various objectives, the key to total institutional quality lies in the effectiveness with which these objectives are reflected and advanced within the institutional goal or mission. An institution has characteristics as a whole that the programs individually may or may not have. At the institutional level, the administrative structures, the adequacy of student support services, the effectiveness of management and resource allocation, and a series of other factors that facilitate or hinder accomplishment of objectives and mission become considerably more crucial. Regardless of the type of institution, a clear determination of mission is essential to assessing whether resources are being used effectively to achieve appropriate educational objectives. But any type of institution is subject to such analysis in light of its unique characteristics. At the institutional level, the balance of programs and program obejctives in the light of mission is essential. This includes both on- and off-campus programs, programs of traditional and nontraditional character, and even provisions for alternatives in achieving specific objectives. There frequently will be tensions between programs and between programs and institutional mission. At the institutional level, hard decisions involving the overall quality of the institution must be made. Unless these decisions are to be made on noneducational, political grounds—in which case quality control becomes questionable—they need to be made in the light of mission and the resources available to accomplish the objectives. An academically strong institution with a weak law school may confront a difficult choice—in order to maintain quality, it must either modify its mission and drop the law school or direct scarce resources toward increased efforts to ensure that the law school meets its objectives.

Focus of Applicability for Accreditation. The concept of quality as achievement in kind is central to the theory and process of accreditation, both institutional and specialized. It is the basis of accreditation's assessment both of quality and of enhancement of quality. As noted earlier, accreditation attests that an institution or program has clearly defined and appropriate objectives, that it maintains conditions under which achievement of these objectives can reasonably be expected, that it appears in fact to be accomplishing these objectives, and that it can reasonably be expected to continue to do so. Thus accreditation recognizes that educational processes are not ends in themselves but means to the end of preparing citizens to cope with life and perform a variety of functions in a complex society.

Recognition of the variety of objectives raises another crucial question in the accrediting context. One part of the definition of educational quality calls for appropriate educational objectives. How do we determine that educational objectives are appropriate? Some critics have argued that basing quality judgments on objectives means that all the objectives that an institution has are equally relevant; thus if the institution or program has preparing thieves as an objective, the only question is how successful it is in doing so. Here the answer depends on social relevance and acceptability as they relate to types of human activity. Clearly, certain socially destructive types of activity are not appropriate educational objectives. Within the acceptable types of activity, what is appropriate educationally is determined by a combination of peer-group and public assessment. The peer-group concept is thus crucial to the self-regulatory character of quality determination, where it guards against idiosyncratic definitions of appropriateness.

Indexes of Quality. Clearly, assessment of educational quality as effective use of resources to achieve appropriate educational objectives has major implications for the nature of standards and for the responsibilities of accrediting associations. It means that some existing indexes of quality either lose their relevance or need to be placed in wider contexts. Reputation, resources, process, and outcomes are some of the ways in which quality has been judged in the past.

Reputation has been used as a basis for ranking institutions and programs. It is a component, although not the only component, in the recent ranking of graduate departments developed by the National Academy of Sciences (1982). Indeed, reputation tended to be the critical factor in earlier studies of this sort. While reputation may be of some value as an index of particularly good or bad programs and may even have some relevance to comparative rankings of outstanding programs, it has little to do with the current quality of the programs in question. Reputation involves a time lag, and actual performance tends to change more rapidly than reputation. Reputation can be based on one aspect of a program—for example, research publications—that has little relevance to effectiveness of the program or institution in enabling students to reach their objectives. Clearly, it relates to the general visibility of an institution or program, so that quality programs that are geographically limited or isolated can go unnoticed. For many institutions and types of institution, the reputational sphere has only peripheral relevance for the quality actually present.

Resources are relevant to quality. However, resources alone are no assurance of quality. What is important is how the resources are used to achieve appropriate educational objectives. An institution can be well endowed and have large and dependable sources of income yet be far from realizing its educational potential. In contrast, an institution with limited resources and clear objectives can through efficiency and dedication use its resources far more effectively in achieving its objectives. While a large but underutilized library may be a point of pride, it is hardly a guarantee of quality education. A highly qualified faculty who devote only minimal time to the teaching-learning function are no guarantee of quality education. Without adequate resources to accomplish its objectives, an institution cannot achieve quality, but the presence of these resources alone does not guarantee that quality education is taking place.

Accreditation has often been criticized as too concerned with processes and input factors and not sufficiently concerned with results. In some cases, this criticism has been valid. Consideration of process without concern for results clearly provides little if any basis for evaluating the process itself. Results are critically important to assessment of quality. Outcomes, both intended and unintended, are what education is all about. In emphasizing objectives and missions, most accrediting associations are increasing the emphasis on outcomes. However, insofar as the outcomes are outcomes of process, the process and the results are clearly germane to each other. Considered in isolation, outcomes are as limited as process.

Nature of Standards. The conception of quality as it relates to process and results has major implications for the nature of the standards that accrediting associations use. Clearly, it means that definitional-prescriptive standards have outgrown their usefulness and that they have little to do with determining educational quality. To the extent that they persist, they do a disservice to institutions, students, and the public. Fixed characteristics do not take into account differences in function and changing processes to achieve sound educational objectives.

Standards must relate to accomplishment of educational objectives, goals, and missions. Their functions are to formulate the factors conducive to and indicative of goal accomplishment. In this sense, they translate indexes of goal accomplishment into characteristics statements relevant to mission accomplishment. In this sense, for example, a standard should be not *Three quarters of the faculty must have a Ph.D.* but rather *Faculty qualifications are commensurate with accomplishing the educational objective.* A standard should not be *The library contains 150,000 volumes* but rather *Library resources are adequate for the types of programs offered and the research expectations of faculty, and they are effectively utilized by students and faculty.* A standard should not be *Students will attend so many laboratory sessions a semester* but rather *Students will demonstrate competencies in specified areas.* Where called for, comparative judgments are possible, but the basis for comparison is the institution's or program's success in achieving appropriate educational objectives.

Relevance to Institutions and Specialized Accrediting Associations. There is a difference, not in theory but in application and development, between the standards of institutional accrediting bodies and the standards of specialized accrediting bodies. An institutional accrediting body is primarily concerned with the characteristics of the institution as a whole, including the way in which its various objectives complement one another in the total institutional mission. The institution must direct its self-study to its total operation and programs. Institutional accreditation does not involve specific review of every program but rather the total context of institutional offerings. Specialized accreditation is concerned with a more limited set of programs or school objectives. On the one hand, these objectives include the institution's commitment to the area in question. On the other hand, they also include the characteristics of the field and the expectations of practitioners and the public for that field. This means that part of what is being assessed in assessments of program effectiveness and integrity is the correlation between institutional objectives and professional objectives. To some extent, this limits the institutional options, but it also ensures, or it should ensure, the integrity of the institution in relation to professional or preprofessional preparation. Finally, the nature of standards as statements of characteristics relevant to accomplishment of objective or mission constitutes a firm basis for cooperation among accrediting associations, both institutional and specialized, in working with institutions to conduct complementary or combined self-studies and evaluations. The full potential for such cooperation has yet to be realized, but important steps in this direction are under way.

Effective Use of Accreditation. Given the evolving history of accreditation and the present concern for the quality of postsecondary education at both the national and local levels, the effective use of accreditation as a self-regulatory means of quality assessment and enhancement by the academic and professional communities has great importance for the future health and welfare of postsecondary education and of the students and public that it serves. Quality in postsecondary education is not something mysterious and the processes for determining whether it exists are neither arcane or unmanageable.

Assurance of institutional and program quality and the credibility both of institutions and programs and of their accrediting activities can be strengthened. To do so will require rapid movement in at least five directions. The first involves the institutions themselves and their participation in and use of the accrediting process. Each institution needs to recognize more fully than many now do that accreditation is directly related to its own self-assessment, planning, and institutional research activities. This applies both to institutional and specialized accreditation. In both cases, the accreditation process is based on assessing the extent to which the institution uses its resources to achieve its mission and its particular appropriate objectives. Thus if accreditation is to fulfill its function and if the institution is to benefit fully from it, the institution must internalize the process and relate it effectively to its own self-analysis, planning, and institutional research activities and cycles.

The second direction involves sustained review by the accrediting associations of their standards and criteria. Any criteria that still reflect the definitional-prescriptive mode must be modified. The primary concern of an accrediting association, whether institutional or specialized, should be the appropriateness of institutional or program objectives and the effectiveness with which these objectives are being realized. Thus each accrediting association should constantly review the validity and reliability or effectiveness of its standards in the light of the conception of educational quality.

The third direction involves increasing the cooperation among accrediting associations in their interactions with one another and with institutions. Efforts in this area should include developing data bases to reduce requests for the same or similar information from different associations. It also includes working with institutions on request to provide joint or sequential reviews and site visits and even common self-studies where applicable.

The fourth direction, both for institutions and for accrediting associations, is clear recognition that the primary function of accreditation is not punitive but supportive of quality maintenance and enhancement. This recognition does not relieve accrediting associations of making negative judgments when they are called for. It does make the major thrust of accreditation the support and reinforcement of the quality of an institution as a whole and of its fulfillment of its particular educational objectives.

The fifth direction is for accrediting associations to expand their educational activities for peer review and site visitors so that these persons clearly understand the character and purposes of the accreditation process. Some associations with well-developed standards related to the concept of quality have used site visitors who operated on considerably different assumptions.

The five directions just outlined are illustrative, not exhaustive. Accreditation has come a long way from its activities in the first year of this century. The issue of quality always will be with us. If we are to strengthen quality in a period of fiscal stringency, variable enrollment, increased competition, and demands for increased accountability, accreditation must continue to evolve.

References

Carnegie Foundation for the Advancement of Teaching. *The Control of the Campus.* Washington, D.C.: Carnegie Foundation for the Advancement of Teaching, 1982.
Kaplan, W. A. *Accrediting Agencies' Legal Responsibilities in Pursuit of the Public Interest.* Washington, D.C.: The Council on Postsecondary Accreditation, 1982.

National Academy of Sciences. *An Assessment of Research Doctorate Programs in the United States: Biological Sciences.* Washington, D.C.: National Academy Press, 1982.

Zook, G. F., and Haggerty, M. E. (Eds.). *The Evaluation of Higher Institutions.* Vol. 1. *Principles of Accrediting Higher Institutions.* Chicago: University of Chicago Press, 1936.

Richard M. Millard is president of the Council on Postsecondary Accreditation.

State policy makers have favored a value-added approach to the determination of educational quality.

State Concerns for Learning: Quality and State Policy

Jeanine Stevens
Bruce D. Hamlett

The legal responsibility for education in the United States rests with the state governments. States are responsible for postsecondary education as well as for elementary and secondary education. Their educational responsibilities include both the incorporation and chartering of eduational institutions as well as the evaluation and review of the educational programs offered by such institutions. In addition, various state boards have established specific educational requirements as a prerequisite to granting certificates and licenses to professionals practicing in certain professions. The methods by which these state responsibilities have been discharged and the extent to which the authority for promoting educational quality has been exercised have varied from state to state. Without question, each state is accountable for the quality of its postsecondary educational program. Generally, however, most states have either delegated this responsibility to nongovernmental accrediting agencies or chosen not to exercise their full authority in this area.

Historically, most states have limited their involvement in postsecondary education to the chartering and incorporation of colleges and universities. Institutional autonomy was the predominant characteristic of higher education during the early period of American history. Educational quality was more a concern of the individual college, with this concern frequently resulting in collegial relationships among faculty in a specific discipline. Consistent with this theme of institutional autonomy, some state higher education institutions, such as the University of California, were established as constitutional universities: They had the same independence as other branches of state government. In other states, institutional autonomy was stressed in the enabling legislation that chartered or created the educational institution. General concerns for educational quality placed the responsibility for institutional review and accreditation with voluntary regional associations. There was only limited involvement by state governments.

The post–World War II expansion in postsecondary enrollments and governmental appropriations and the period of campus dissent and disruption that followed led to increased government demands for greater institutional accountability. The rapid expansion of federally funded financial assistance programs, with the changing emphasis from institutional aid to student aid, increased the demand for quality review of the postsecondary institutions that participated in these programs.

During the past two decades, four themes have received increasing attention: federal eligibility, institutional accountability, consumer protection, and educational quality. Response to these themes has included expanded activity in governance and coordination at the state level and continued reliance on nongovernmental accreditation as a prime criterion for institutional eligibility for participation in publicly funded student assistance programs. A fundamental purpose of both activities is to identify, maintain, and promote quality in postsecondary education. The discussion presented in this chapter focuses on state activities, particularly those in California, and on the impact of state activities on quality in education.

A Definition of Quality

With concern over quality in education increasing, a number of methods have been used to measure quality, including such traditional approaches as examining an institution's reputation and resources, and such recent measures as outcomes (a favorite of educators) and the value-added, student-oriented, and action-oriented approaches (Astin, 1982). Others argue that quality cannot be defined, and perhaps a commonsense approach is best. "Quality is good carpentry, good plumbing, good poetry... the determination of faculty members, deans, [and]... presidents to transcend themselves to reach higher than their grasp" (Enarson, 1983, p. 8).

The most basic definitions of quality for colleges and universities is the one used by the Commission on Colleges and Universities of the North Central Association of Colleges and Secondary Schools. This definition states that students "receive a fair education for their investment of time and money." This value-added or institutional-impact definition of quality, which is favored by educators and policy makers, involves a return investment: Students, taxpayers, benefactors, or anyone else who pays for education gets a fair return on the resources invested. When state agencies use this definition to judge quality, they look at both excellence and efficiency of educational operations: not only the value added by the competence that students gain during their enrollment and by their level of competence at graduation but also by the efficient use of resources in helping students to develop this competence.

Operations by state as well as nongovernmental accrediting agencies to review the quality of educational programs and institutions require the measurement of both excellence and efficiency. Students' growth of competence and level of competence at graduation and efficient use of resources must all be assessed. Neither an institution that wastes its resources nor an institution that wastes the time and effort of students is an institution of quality.

The Role of Statewide Agencies

Most states have assigned the responsibility for quality review to a specific state governmental agency. For example, in California, the Postsecondary Education Commission has the responsibility to develop criteria for evaluating the effectiveness of all aspects of postsecondary education. In Colorado, the Commission on Higher Education has the responsibility to effect the best utilization of available resources so as to achieve an adequate level of higher education in the most economic manner. In Connecticut, the Board of Higher Education is required to maintain standards of quality ensuring a position of national leadership for state institutions of higher education. In Pennsylvania, in order to assure the maintenance of the quality of state-owned colleges and universities, each institution is subject to periodic visits by the Secretary of Education, and in West Virginia, the board of regents makes rules and regulations for the accreditation of all colleges and other institutions of higher education in the state.

Statewide planning and coordinating agencies are in a unique position to monitor developments in all sectors of postsecondary education and to place particular emphasis on the maintenance of quality in public institutions. In a review of state-level planning agencies, Glenny (1959) argued that effective state planning by these agencies should contribute to adequate diversity in types of educational institutions and programs, appropriate designation and maintenance of differential functions among the several types and systems of institutions, and appropriate allocation of resources and support to the units of a coordinated system.

A second major study of statewide coordinating boards (Glenny and others, 1971) emphasized the role of the coordinating boards as an intermediary between the state government and institutions of higher education. Effectiveness was contingent on the objectivity of the coordinating agencies and on their ability to maintain the confidence of both higher education and state government. The authors argued that coordinating boards had a number of additional functions or "essential powers" for effective operations, including continuous long- and short-range planning, a statewide data system for collecting information from all postsecondary education institutions, program review, budget review, and administration of state and federal scholarship and grant programs. The authors considered these powers essential to ensure against domination of public higher education by the executive branch of state government.

While pressure for the establishment of statewide coordinating boards began in the 1950s and 1960s during a time of budgetary and enrollment expansion, the final push for their existence did not occur until passage of the Education Amendments Act of 1982, which amended the Higher Education Act of 1965: Section 1202 requires any state wanting federal funds to establish or designate a state postsecondary commission representing public, private, nonprofit, and proprietary postsecondary institutions. In response to the Education Amendments, the planning activities of existing agencies were broadened, and states that lacked a coordinating agency established one. Because the Education Amendments expanded the definition of higher education to include all postsecondary education, the private vocational and technical schools as well as the independent colleges and universities were represented on the state boards and commissions together with their counterparts from the public sectors. Presently, every state has some type of coordinating board or 1202 commission responsible for postsecondary education. Although there is great variability in specific functions and organization, all these commissions have planning and coordinating activities, and all are therefore concerned with the effectiveness and efficiency of postsecondary education within the state.

The planning and research activities of the coordinating boards change as the predominant educational issues of society at large change, particularly when those changes seem to affect or threaten the quality of education. In cooperation with representatives of the State Higher Education Executive Officers (SHEEO), the Education Commission of the States produces a yearly summary of issues considered by the statewide coordinating boards and their recommendations for solutions to problems resulting from these issues. It is interesting to note that the two major issues considered by state coordinating agencies during the expansion and growth of higher education in the 1950s — avoidance of duplication and effective use of resources — are the same issues now being considered in current efforts to plan for enrollment declines and the increased financial pressure caused by inflation. Millard (1976) comments that institutions often find it convenient to use the statewide coordinating boards as a scapegoat because the inducement for cooperation from institutions is gone as funding drops and costs increase. Consequently, he considers it crucial to involve institutions in agency activities to guard against political intervention. The role of the state boards has become increasingly difficult as they seek to promote both efficiency in the use of limited resources and excellence in educational programs. Educational planning must deal with the fact of limited resources while also meeting the demands for academic accountability, evaluation, and quality in student and teacher performance.

Program Review Activities of the States: A Quality Assessment

Program review is one of the major methods that state coordinating boards use to promote quality in educational programs. This activity has increased in importance as the influence of the boards themselves has grown. Recommendations have been made for state boards to review public institutions to determine their progress toward state goals; these reviews can become a basis for budget allocations (Marcus and others, 1983). The legal basis for program review varies from state to state, depending on whether it is derived from statutory or from budgetary authority. Program review is ultimately linked with planning and budgetary review. Barak and Berdahl (1978) stress that possession of statutory authority to review academic programs does not indicate how extensive this review actually is. Agencies sometimes find that their review activities are limited by staff resources. Absence of explicit statutory responsibility to review programs may not prevent such activity, however, as agencies that lack such authority have conducted such reviews.

Criteria most frequently used in program review are productivity (degrees awarded), cost per program graduate, quality (as relected by national or regional reputation), and need (general student interest or demand trends). While quality is listed as a major criterion for program review, most state review agencies resist the quality and quantity emphasis for two reasons: Criteria based on quantity deny the goals and objectives of higher education, and criteria based on quality place faculty on the defensive; many faculty stress that quality depends on the resources of a university (Melchiori, 1982).

California's Education Code requires the state's postsecondary education commission to do two things: first, to review programs proposed by the three public segments (University of California, California State University, and the California community colleges) and make recommendations regarding such proposals to the legislature and the governor; second, in consultation with the public segments, to establish a schedule for segmental review of selected existing programs (including standards directed at quality control), evaluation of this review process, and report of the findings. The commission considers program review a serious activity because recommendations for elimination of programs are inherent in the process. However, the commission "has not considered the elimination of certain numbers of programs each year an appropriate or necessary goal for the campus review process." Instead, it "regards the periodic review of each program as a safeguard—if reductions must be made—against arbitrary and ill considered programmatic decisions" (California Postsecondary Education Commission, 1983, p. 5).

Program review, as conducted by the California statewide coordinating board, is considered to be qualitative in a broad sense: An institution must ensure that a program has the appropriate curriculum and qualified faculty. Overall quality determinations are left up to the segmental or campus reviews, with the Commission monitoring that process as an advisory body that leaves final decisions up to the segmental offices. The staff of the statewide boards are in large part generalists in education, and the final determination of the quality of a particular program requires a specialist in the field. Thus statewide staff tend to rely on segmental review of programs with the expectation that it will be a review of quality involving such expertise as may be necessary. For new programs, the California Postsecondary Education Commission relies on the judgment of segmental offices; for existing programs, it relies on adherence to established campus standards or criteria as a measure of quality. Moreover, like many other statewide coordinating agencies, the commission reviews programs to determine whether they have a market demand. This is not considered to be a qualitative judgment.

The argument that reductions in programs threaten the quality of an institution or the academic integrity of a geographic region is still unresolved. One study may argue that reductions in course offerings necessitated by leveling enrollments and funding is harmful to program quality, while another may state that new graduate programs can threaten the quality of existing programs in a region by producing an oversupply of Ph.D.'s. The evidence does not indicate that savings are achieved through program review and subsequent reduction of programs, since many programs recommended for termination are marginal in the sense that they are low-cost, low-enrollment offerings that provide easy targets for review panels.

In addition to the state coordinating boards, systemwide administrative offices attempt to ensure quality education through a variety of procedures, including program review, reviews of teacher competence and student academic achievement, state-mandated reviews, and other types of ongoing studies. For example, the University of California's program review—a fairly complicated process—is considered by some systemwide administrators to be a more rigorous method for achieving quality than the accreditation process. Reviews are made when resource constraints call for a reduction or intercampus consolidation of programs or when it seems that a program offered on a few campuses should be offered on additonal campuses. A 1982 plan called for a selective reduction of programs rather than across-the-board cuts that could threaten the quality of all programs. Program review by the university led to the discontinuation of eight degree programs and two certificate programs during the 1981-82 academic year.

The California State University's program review process is conducted periodically by faculty to make certain that the programs maintain integrity and that they are worthwhile. Regional accreditation is considered by systemwide staff to constitute another assurance of quality. If a state university wants to expand an existing program, the program must be accredited by a specialized accrediting agency to ensure that what is proposed is recognized and endorsed by peers. Individual campuses conduct other types of reviews, ideally using educational specialists from outside California. According to a recent report from the Chancellor's Office of the State University (Morey, 1983, p. 99), "program review is essential to ensure the continued enhancement of the quality of academic programs and the flexibility of the academic enterprise. It can provide some judgment about the worth and needs of a program.... The development and maintenance of excellence in academic programs is dependent upon the continuous monitoring and periodic change that are part of the program review process."

At most public colleges and universities, the program review process usually involves the interplay of four formal procedures. For example, for teacher education programs in California, all public colleges and universities are reviewed by the Western Association of Schools and Colleges, which periodically (usually every ten years) assesses the educational quality of the entire institution. Second, the teacher education programs on many campuses are reviewed and accredited by the National Council for the Accreditation of Teacher Education (NCATE), which is the major national accrediting agency for professional education. A third review is conducted by the State Commission for Teacher Credentialing, which was established in 1970 with the charge of "insuring excellence in education by encouraging high standards of quality and diversity" (Morey, 1983, p. 99). Fourth, the systemwide administration reviews every campus program every five years. Systemwide staff report that these reviews can and most frequently do include consideration of the purposes and goals of a program, its curricular content, human and material resources, past and current accomplishments, program graduates, and general and specific strengths and weaknesses. This four-level review process is typical of most postsecondary academic institutions. The assumption is usually that educational quality is promoted by the process. Many educators argue, however, that frequent program reviews by different agencies consume considerable staff time and effort, which is actually debilitating to the programs.

Accreditation and Quality

Accreditation emerges time and again in discussions of state-level review of quality in postsecondary education. While there are some differences of opinion about the degree to which accreditation measures, ensures, or promotes quality, states rely heavily on the accreditation process as a way of reviewing program quality and of determining effective use of resources at postsecondary institutions. State licensure boards also frequently use accreditation as one important requirement for the granting of professional licenses or certificates.

While states have the responsibility for assuring that licensed professionals are adequately trained and skilled, most licensing boards rely on accreditation as a measure of institutional or program quality. A state board or agency may actually review some institutions or programs (in California: barber examiners, certified shorthand reporters, state bar) and in other areas rely on accreditation as the primary criterion. There is a great diversity in the requirements for professional licensure or certification in California, but for at least thirteen professions, particularly in the health-related professions, graduation from an accredited school is essential. Thus to say that the state is using a value-added approach in looking at the effective and efficient use of resources is to be only partly correct. State licensing boards and systemwide administrative offices also rely on regional and specialized accreditation for that purpose.

Summary

States have legal responsibility for education, including program evaluation and review. A number of state agencies conduct a general review process to evaluate programs for efficiency and effectiveness and to guard against program duplication. State agencies can also rely on accreditation as a marker of educational quality, thus partly delegating their responsibility to private voluntary organizations. Lawrence and Green (1980) characterize accreditation and state program review as external approaches to quality assessment in higher education, which they contrast with internal or campus-based academic reviews. Both kinds of review are necessary, because each takes a unique approach to quality assessment. Accreditation focuses on capacity and achievement. Assessments are noncompetitive in that no ranking of institutions or programs is done by accrediting agencies. State concerns for quality in education focus on review of resource allocations, access, consumer protection, and productivity. Both these external approaches add another measure to the total picture of efforts to determine educational quality. States may rely on accreditation partly because of the different criteria used and partly because of the high cost of institutional reviews to the state. While state policy makers and educators have favored a value-added approach to determinations of quality, they often lack the budgetary resources necessary for the activities—collecting and analyzing data over a number of years—that would allow them to determine whether educational quality exists.

The California state coordinating agency considers assessment of the quality of academic and vocational programs and the means used for establishing, maintaining, and improving such quality to be one major goal for the 1980s. In the past, program review has been limited by existing policies and fiscal constraints. Therefore, the educational reviews conducted by California state coordinating boards and commissions and other state agencies can assess quality in only a general and limited manner. Rather than assessing quality, these reviews may have done little more than monitor and attempt to coordinate the various pieces of the postsecondary education puzzle. Nevertheless, a special measure of quality comes through this review, coordination, and subsequent planning process. By their impartiality, the state boards bring a balance to postsecondary education. Of course, the ideal is to have leadership not only identify, assess, and maintain quality but also promote and create it. This is most likely to occur at the campus level, but the state, through watchful coordination and planning, can serve as a cautionary system to alert policy makers, educators, and faculty to areas in postsecondary education in which quality may be in jeopardy. This adds another essential dimension to reviews of educational quality by other state agencies, academic systemwide offices, governing boards, and campus educators.

References

Astin, A. W. "Why Not Try Some New Ways of Measuring Quality?" *Educational Record,* 1982, *63* (2), 10-15.

Barak, R. J., and Berkahl, R. O. *State-Level Academic Program Review in Higher Education.* Denver: Education Commission of the States, 1978.

California Postsecondary Education Commission. *Annual Summary of Program Review Activities, 1981-82.* Sacramento: California Postsecondary Education Commission, 1983.

Enarson, H. L. "Quality — Indefinable but Not Unattainable." *Educational Record,* 1983, *64* (1), 7-9.

Glenny, L. A., Berdahl, R. O., Palola, E. G., and Paltridge, J. G. *Coordinating Higher Education for the Seventies.* Berkeley, Calif.: Center for Research and Development in Higher Education, 1971.

Glenny, L. A. *Autonomy of Public Colleges: The Challenge of Coordination.* New York: McGraw-Hill, 1959.

Lawrence, J. K., and Green, K. C. *A Question of Quality: The Higher Education Ratings Game.* AAHE-ERIC Higher Education Research Report no. 5. Washington, D.C.: American Association for Higher Education, 1980.

Marcus, L. K., Leone, A. O., and Goldberg, E. D. *The Path to Excellence: Quality Assurance in Higher Education.* ASHE-ERIC Higher Education Research Report no. 1. Washington, D.C.: Association for the Study of Higher Education, 1983.

Melchiori, G. S. *Planning for Program Discontinuance: From Default to Design.* AAHE-ERIC Higher Education Research Report no. 5. Washington, D.C.: American Association for Higher Education, 1982.

Millard, R. C. *State Boards of Higher Education.* ERIC Higher Education Research Report no. 4. Washington, D.C.: American Association for Higher Education, 1976.

Morey, A. I. *Excellence in Professional Education: A Report of the Advisory Committee to Study Programs in Education in the California State University.* Long Beach: Office of the Chancellor, California State University, 1983.

Jeanine Stevens and Bruce D. Hamlett are postsecondary education specialists for the California Postsecondary Education Commission, where they work on accreditation and student affirmative action.

Standards are expectations about performance, and as such they precede issues of assessment.

The Major Seventh: Standards as a Leading Tone in Higher Education

Clifford Adelman

For eighteen months, I served on partial detail from the National Institute of Education to assist the National Commission on Excellence in Education. My intention here is to report some of what we learned during that time that bears on the agenda of higher education and, more importantly, to offer at least one analytic framework in which the learning can be placed.

In its inquiry, the commission came to understand American education as a continuum that extends far beyond the formal system of schools and colleges. But within the formal system there appeared to be six key standards that are set principally by institutions of higher education: standards of content in the disciplines and the interdisciplines; standards for the level of academic performance expected of students—which are not actuarial or arbitrary standards; standards for the use and allocation of time for academic

This article is an adaptation and expansion of a talk presented to the 1983 annual conference of the American Association for Higher Education. It is offered by the author in his individual capacity as an associate at the National Institute of Education. It should not be taken to reflect the judgments or opinions of the National Institute of Education, the National Commission on Excellence in Education or any of the Commissioners, or the U.S. Department of Education.

learning, a set of critical variables affecting learning that, as we discovered, has comparatively little to do with the traditional academic calendar; standards for the preparation of teachers at all levels of education and standards for the treatment of teachers as professionals; standards of cooperation with schools, industry, government, and other institutions for the improvement of education and the advancement of knowledge; and standards for the behavior of institutions that is subject to ethical and value judgment.

I want to develop the first two of these standards—content and student performance—in terms of the commission's findings. I will cover the other four in the course of explaining those findings.

The terms of this analysis should be clear. My first distinction is between requirements and standards, a simple but extraordinarily important distinction given the cacophony that pervades contemporary discussions of American education. The term *requirements* refers strictly to time on subject matter and the presentation of credentials. When we say that a student must take four years of English in high school or thirty-six credits of liberal arts courses in college, we are talking about requirements, not standards. When we say that a student must present a high school diploma to qualify for college admission or that a student must take a placement examination in English composition before moving from the sophomore to the junior year of college, we are also talking about requirements. The language of requirements, unlike that of standards, is a language of imperatives.

In contrast, the term *standards* is a buzzword, and I want to replace the buzz with something analogous to the major seventh interval in music. The major seventh is a leading tone—it establishes expectations—and standards are a form of expectations that refer to performance. We use measures to determine whether expectations are being met, and we set benchmarks along those measures to indicate the level of performance that we expect on the measure. If we use the term *standards* correctly, then, the language of standards is a language of performance, of outcomes.

It is obvious that some measures of performance are easier to establish than others and that some benchmarks are easier to set than others. It is difficult, for example, to measure interorganizational cooperations, and some people would argue that the measurement of ethical behavior of institutions is a moot question because individuals behave; institutions do not. But, an institution's statement of expectations is itself a performance that is subject to judgment. In Trow's (1975, p. 124) terms, the "public life" of institutions is very much open to measurement, while such factors of the "private life" of institutions as "the human qualities of students and teachers, the social and psychological processes of teaching and learning, and the individual and social gains and benefits of higher education" are not.

The initial point of contention is that, to the extent that colleges and universities fail to set and maintain high standards in each category, to the extent that they fail to make their measures and benchmarks of performance clear to us all, the entire educational system suffers.

The evidence gathered by the commission suggests strongly that the current report card on higher education in America is, at best, mixed, and that too many of our 3,300 institutions of higher education are not maintaining the standards of time, content, expectations, cooperation, and ethical behavior commensurate with their responsibilities.

The positive aspects of the report card should also be cited, even to those well versed in them. When the commission looked back across the past quarter century of American education, there was no question that postsecondary institutions had undergone a tremendous transformation and that, on the whole, they had adapted well to both growth and an increasingly diverse constituency. It is particularly important not to lose the lessons and sensitivities of that transformation because, as Blake (1982) pointed out to the commission, the future of higher education will be driven even more than it now is by the demography of those new constituencies. If the higher education that we offer to women, to older adults, to minorities, and to the geographically isolated falls short of their expectations and does not improve their capacity to perform, then access will have been an absolute sham.

Standards of Content

Sham is a strong word, yet some of our findings suggest that the word can be applied — if selectively — to the current situation. For example, over the past decade, colleges and universities developed remedial and supportive service programs for underprepared students that proved very successful in rectifying — in a remarkably short time — some of the basic deficiencies in students' previous schooling. But it was unclear from the evidence that we examined whether colleges persisted in moving these students beyond the old basics or beyond the most elementary study skills. It appeared as if many of our colleges said, in effect, "Well, now that you have passed Study Skills 101, Remedial Math, and Remedial English and attended our orientation workshops for a semester, you're just fine, and we'll see you next in Advanced Inorganic Chemistry." Failure to persist in the real mission of equity, failure to follow through, is to generate the conditions of a shipwreck that underprepared students will not survive.

Likewise, what we found particularly fascinating in examining selected innovative programs in postsecondary science and mathematics education was that they emphasized process rather than content. Thus, college students may simply be learning outmoded material in more efficient ways. This unhappy paradox indicates that the standards of content may have been neglected. The current rage for computer literacy and the slightly mellowed rage for computer-assisted instruction (CAI) are prime examples of this triumph of process. If physics courses relying heavily of CAI are limited to the subject matter of mechanics and neglect quantum electrodynamics, if the software for CAI-dependent biology courses is dominated by order, genus, and species, and neglects molecular biology, then students may learn some stuff, but it is not the right stuff for the current state of these disciplines. And when a college defines computer literacy as the student's ability to retrieve information on the student's current course schedule, interim course grades, and credit—a task about as demanding as operating a quotron terminal at a brokerage house or using an automated teller at a bank—then we are not establishing standards of content for higher learning commensurate with the human capacity for higher-order cognitive operations.

In a disciplinary context, standards of content represent a consensus of facts, cognitive operations, and knowledge of resources necessary to manipulate and understand sets of unknowns subject to investigation within the context of the discipline. What does it mean, for example, to write a history of the American economy in the early decades of this century? Historians should be able to agree on the concepts, techniques, sources, and alternative interpretive frameworks that students should know in order to accomplish that task. And if our ability to classify, store, and retrieve complex economic and social data has advanced to the point at which the objects of knowledge are accessible within the time we allocate for learning history, then it is reasonable to require the content of a course or program to include them. We can then measure the quality of the course or program against the articulation of that knowledge.

Standards of Academic Performance

The bottom line in assessing the effectiveness of any educational institution lies in the achievement and performance of students. The commission and its staff found it odd that large-scale research on growth and change in college students, with a few dated exceptions (Hyman and others, 1975), has focused on every conceivable topic other than students' academic learning and that the nation has never undertaken a comprehensive pulse reading of college student learning analogous to the National Assessment of Educational Progress. If measurements of educational progress come to a screeching halt when people reach the age of seventeen, we give the false impression—incommensurate with the goals of a learning society—that education and learning stop at that age. Despite the absence of a comprehensive measure, scores provided by Educational Testing Service and the College Board on standardized tests taken by college graduates indicate declines in achievement greater than those for high school graduates.

Why have we not noticed this very disturbing trend? Or, better still, why have we not bothered to notice it? The data are accessible; and while I am sure that the "test lawyers" would offer their usual reams of comments on every score, the evidence of commonsense empiricism is fairly strong. Since 1965, for example, there has been a 16 percent decline in scores on the verbal section of the Graduate Record Examination (GRE), compared to a 14 percent decline on the Scholastic Aptitude Test (SAT) verbal tests. Moreover, a score on the Graduate Record Examination achievement tests in such subjects as English and history have declined approximately 15 percent, while scores in comparable fields on the College Board achievement tests have remained relatively stable. Finally, performance on the Graduate Management Admissions Test, which picks up the huge increase in undergraduate business administration majors, has fallen by 6 percent.

Now, these are admittedly selective data (the Law School Admission Test scores, for example, have gone up), and we must always be wary of presenting the judgments of test data in such a raw form. But other evidence presented to the commission corroborated these trends. Most significantly, in terms of the performance of community college and four-year college graduates in occupational skills, we received ample testimony from employers concerning the necessity for retraining college graduates in subjects ranging from foreign languages to finance, from matrix algebra to communications skills of all kinds. We are very effective, they told the commissioners, at identifying college graduates who do not know whether the calculator they are using is functioning properly and equally effective at determining which of those students still think that Latin American is one country. The fact that employers are compelled to retrain—for reasons other than orientation to organizational norms—indicates that the college degree is no longer a reliable indicator of competence.

While it may be possible to retrain college graduates in skills and knowledge that they should have acquired in secondary school and reinforced in college, other expected outcomes of postsecondary education are more difficult to address in corporate education programs. What are these outcomes, these expectations? Testimony to the commission from large employers, such as Xerox, CIGNA, Standard Oil of Indiana, Continental Illinois Bank, the U.S. Department of State, and others, persistently cited a twofold set of characteristics: first, such generic mental capacities as the ability to look for, identify and undertake an analysis of change, regardless of field; an understanding of the nature of evidence and of what constitutes adequate evidence in the several broad areas of knowledge; holistic and creative thinking abilities; and differential perspective (that is, the ability to set existing knowledge and analysis in new contexts); and second, such generic traits or attitudes as adaptability and tolerance for ambiguity and complexity, the ability to learn and work in groups, persistence in coming to closure on an idea or issue, and enthusiasm for work. If colleges and universities truly seek to educate the whole person, they must inevitably address the development of these capacities, traits, and attitudes—not for the sake of service to an employer but for the sake of maintaining their own public standards for student learning and growth.

However, in the course of our work, we found very few two- or four-year colleges that required a student to demonstrate true proficiency in anything as a condition for receiving a degree, fewer still that set clear learning objectives and unambiguous standards for academic performance in undergraduate programs, and only a handful that measured the value that their programs added to student capacities and knowledge between entrance and graduation. In addition, when we examined more than 200 profiles of notable programs and promising approaches in higher education, only a third of those who wrote the profiles seemed to know what questions to ask in assessing the success of their own program.

It should not surprise us, of course, that we do not measure college student learning. As Astin (1982, p. 9) has observed, college administrators rarely refer to student learning as part of the operation that they run; and their management information systems provide them "with feedback on budgets, enrollments, course loads, and physical plant and facilities but say practically nothing about the education progress or development of students." Looking across all our evidence, then—it is much broader than what I have cited here suggests—we had to ask what accounts for the mixed report card. A number of factors, including the four other standards listed earlier, enlightened our assessment.

Requirements, Standards, and the Market Model

The budgets of most colleges are driven by enrollments, and both admission and graduation requirements (not standards) have been diluted to prop up enrollment. The effects on the course-taking behaviors of high school students are staggering (Adelman, 1982), and colleges cannot blame the schools for deficiencies in student preparation under conditions of that influence. However, when colleges recently decided to show somebody that they meant business, what did they do vis-à-vis admissions? The first instinct was to juggle admissions standards, not requirements. For example, Florida State University raised the SAT cutoff score to 950 and the minimum high school grade point average (GPA) to 2.5; the Oregon state system raised the minimum acceptable high school GPA .25 across the board; and the University of Texas at Austin increased the minimum SAT cutoff score from 800 to 1,100, principally to slow enrollment growth. (Other institutions should enjoy that luxury!) These arbitrary actuarial responses do nothing for the quality of education in the system.

We can make some excuses for public institutions in this regard, as the level of state aid influences admissions standards. That is, in light of declining real-dollar appropriations, the only way to reduce costs is to reduce enrollment, and the easiest way to reduce enrollment is to juggle the actuarial tables. This is an odd kind of market mechanism, but perhaps we ought to look at it more closely.

At one time, students paid college lecturers directly. This fee system, which operated in Europe up to the sixteenth century, was about as close to the pure market model as higher education ever came. When the number of institutions was limited, the focus of the market was on the instructor. Students bought learning—or so one assumed. A large segment of higher education in the United States today is also market-driven, but in a different sense.

Through federally supported student loan programs, a significant percentage of our undergraduates receives what is in effect a public entitlement. This entitlement represents our acceptance of the validity of the human capital thesis (Becker, 1964). What has changed is the seller: Students now buy from institutions, not from teachers, and as long as that model prevails, colleges become more akin to utilitarian organizations and less akin to normative organizations. The locus of standards thus changes: from the control of the institution to the control of the market. As Bowen (1975, p. 9) has wisely observed, the more closely colleges are geared to the labor market, the more they are "in danger of becoming merely an instrument of forces that would weaken democracy and subvert individual freedom." Why? Because education for a job (as opposed to education for life's work) restricts both the awareness of personal choice and the development of critical citizenship.

It is ironic that our institutions' first instincts in regaining control focused on the symbolic numbers of test scores and GPAs. But in light of the fact that, according to the College Board, SAT scores and GPAs individually or together do not predict college grades as well as the combination of SAT and achievement test scores, one must interpret those instincts as cued to the market, not to learning.

Standards for Allocation of Time

Given the search for enrollments and the time-based nature of college degrees, the credit system has been abused in many colleges and universities. When, as we found, a state university grants as much credit for a course called Hi-Fi Systems for the Music Lover as it does for college algebra or communication theory, when another offers more credit for a course called Basic Nature Photography than it does for courses in neuropsychology or American diplomatic history, then standards for the allocation of time for academic learning have been lowered. As long as the college credit system equates allocated time with learning and bases its values on class contact hours, we will have continued problems with standards because our credit system states our values. And students—both current and prospective—are very sensitive to the messages that we unwittingly send.

By using the credit system as an accounting mechanism, not as an indication of academic value, colleges and universities have generated mass confusion between credentials and education, encouraging the accumulation of chits rather than learning. The cynicism that students develop under such circumstances is pervasive: It is as standard a feature of registration desks for business administration majors at state colleges as it is of the highly competitive preprofessional programs in selective liberal arts colleges. What does it take to get by? What does it take to accumulate the requisite number of chits in the appropriate places?

Degree Programs

To attract students with mistaken notions of the relationship between education and vocation, colleges and universities have tolerated an excess of vocational and preprofessional curricula of very narrow scope, and they have allowed students too much latitude to focus only on their major and specialized allied courses. The study of college student transcripts in the early 1970s by Blackburn and others (1976) more than adequately demonstrates the disparity between the catalogue curriculum and the curriculum experienced by students. And when the community college system of one state offers no less than 197 occupational degree programs ranging from horseshoing to operating room technician (London, 1982), it becomes clear that higher education has lost control over the standards of content that lie behind degrees.

Some community colleges will argue that they are enhancing the socially desirable goal of access by offering a great number of degree programs. But, Hyde (1982) has argued persuasively that such factors as the number of sites and times of day at which courses and programs are offered is far more important to the enhancement of access than the diversity of offerings. If that is the case, colleges can focus on a limited number of programs at times and sites convenient to potential student populations. Proximity, Hyde (1982, p. 91) demonstrates, has a significant impact on enrollment, particularly on enrollment of blacks; thus, he argues, "elements of access and quality may be pursued jointly rather than being viewed as goals competing for the same resources."

Curricular Coherence

Despite recent movements toward reform, most undergraduate curricula remain fragmented. We have created programs that call themselves *disciplines*, although the only object of their discipline is departmental organization. The more such programs in a college or university and the more their advocates in faculty senates and administrations can claim the status of a particular working of mind or a discrete body of knowledge, the more they grasp an organizational niche, and the more diffuse the entire enterprise becomes.

There is, then a surface of organizational claims in our colleges and universities beneath which we ask the student to perceive coherence. But the student moves through a landscape of time and content, going from a class in chemistry to a class in communication, then on to a class in "police science." All these are called disciplines, all have departments, and all struggle to survive a battle for resources and enrollments that has little to do with learning. As a counterpoint, the public statements of colleges and universities lay claim to a common learning, an ineffable something that students are expected to perceive as providing coherence. It seems, however, that no matter how we strive to explicate the essence of that desired learning, the more incoherent the student's experience becomes.

Take, for example, the noble notions that our common learning should include knowledge and perspectives about women and non-Western cultures and knowledge of the ethical and social dimensions of science and technology. So, what do we do? A decade ago, we took the separatist approach: We created new programs—women's studies, international studies, black studies, and what the medical and nursing schools called health care humanities. Subsequently, we discovered that strategy was self-reflexive: Women took women's studies courses, blacks took black studies courses, and doctors and nurses took health care humanities. No one else did. There was no common learning of the sort that we desired.

Our second approach was integrationist, built along lines similar to those informing the writing-across-the-curriculum movement. That is, we decided to "feminize" the curriculum, to "internationalize" the curriculum, to "computerize" the curriculum—simultaneously. In so doing, we laid tremendous responsibilities on faculty in a very short time, and in the process, we expected students to perceive what we were doing by osmosis. Documents examined by the commission indicate that, while it may be possible to assess the impact of discrete thrusts of this integrationist approach on student attitudes and assumptions, no one has attempted a comprehensive measure of its cumulative impact on student learning.

What we did not do in all this was to make any attempt to understand who our students were. One reason why most colleges cannot achieve curricular coherence is that they do not establish a baseline inventory of entering students' knowledge, learning behaviors, levels of competence in various cognitive operations, and assumptions about the scene of postsecondary education. Measures and benchmarks of both content and performance are built on such inventories, yet we tend to denigrate the institutional research and faculty participation necessary to establish them.

Communication: What Students Do Not Know

The commission was advised by both counselors and students themselves that most entering college freshmen have little idea of what the transition from secondary to postsecondary education means and of what is expected of them as academic workers—if you will—and young adults. With few but notable exceptions, our institutions of higher education have failed to address this critical stage in the lives of students.

To address the problems that students have with that transition involves establishing standards for communicating knowledge concerning collegiate settings, institutional processes, and expectations for academic work. For example, we assume that the vast majority of entering freshmen can discriminate among the types of credentials offered by colleges and universities. My experience in administering the American Council on Education/Cooperative Institutional Research Program's annual survey of entering freshmen for five years in a state college is that they do not. There are two questions on the survey that ask, in sequence, What is the highest degree you intend to receive? and, What is the highest degree you intend to receive from this institution? In nearly one out of three cases, students gave a higher answer to the second question than they did to the first, and another 10 percent could not answer either question. Yet we place incredible pressure on students to embark on a transition that requires such knowledge. In the words of a college admissions counselor who testified to the commission (Mazzuca, 1982), these students "do not know what they do not know — they are asked to declare a major for a field they know nothing about, choose a school from pictures in brochures, sort through an alphabet maze of acronyms, and fill out form after form for a career they probably will not enter five years down the line."

No one has been negotiating reality with the majority of students who enter our postsecondary institutions each year, and we have yet to understand that, in the absence of clear and comprehensive communication, students will turn to the most easily accessible structure in a college in which to negotiate for themselves — the major. If we complain that students overspecialize on entrance to college and that this tendency is a result of vocationalism, we miss the point. The fault is ours. The student is seeking academic and personal identity, and as one college freshman remarked to the commissioners, the largest concern for freshmen is reestablishing an identity. If we do not assist that process with clear information and strong guidance, by the end of the freshman year students will construct an image of postsecondary learning as an uninspiring rite of passage that they must endure. They will then simplify the rite by focusing on the major and hence prevent the discovery of self and the articulation of their own values and options.

This, if our postsecondary institutions genuinely believe that they are educating the whole person — the statement is often made in their catelogues — they must start communicating far earlier with their prospective students. The barrier we face in this regard, however, is formidable: The most credible resource at our disposal for engaging in that communication, our faculty, has neither the training nor the incentive to do so.

Standards of Cooperation: The Lack of Incentives

There are insufficient incentives and rewards for college faculty to engage in sustained dialogue with and outreach to secondary schools and other educational institutions. The standards of cooperation among institutions engaged in a common enterprise thus cannot be maintained. Perhaps I am overly cynical, but it strikes me that public awards for excellence in teaching or community service are, at many of our colleges, hollow rituals that deflect tensions that might otherwise arise in the tenure and promotion process.

Colleges and universities are normative institutions in which an ideal of rationality and an admiration for disciplinary technique prevail. In order to establish productive interorganizational relationships with other types of institutions, we have to do something that we now too rarely do: stretch to imagine other ideals and norms, then achieve a degree of negative capability. What does it mean, for example, to live in a utilitarian organization in which multidisciplinary decision making is the dominant mode and teams are the dominant form of organization? In other words, what is it like to live in a large corporation? If we can find ways to encourage faculty to stretch, we can work with other types of organizations. The same type of analogy can be offered in the case of secondary schools, where the mandate for intersectoral communication is strong.

Eliminating unnecessary repetitions within the system calls for close cooperation between postsecondary and secondary education in particular. While the commission saw a number of commendable efforts in that direction, it focused principally on the question of the courses that should be required in secondary schools, not on the standards of content of those courses, the academic work habits expected of students in postsecondary institutions, or adequate information concerning credentials and careers. That commissions in such states as Ohio, California, and Wisconsin worked with secondary school teachers and administrators to develop statements of competences expected from specific courses of study indicates that there is hope for wide-scale cooperation. But there is a public posture and a private life to such developments: Intervention by commission without a reward system that encourages college and school faculty to continue to monitor and improve content and communication between the sectors may well create the conditions of future benign neglect. In this case, we do not get performance without a professional incentive.

Standards for the Preparation of Faculty

Most four-year college faculty receive no training whatsoever as teachers, and they seem to pick up whatever they know about student development, curriculum, or assessment by osmosis during their early years of teaching. There is no quality control in that. Our student body is far more diverse, and colleges as organizations are for more complex than they were a scant twenty years ago, yet we are preparing our future faculty only as disciplinary experts and in ways that basically have not changed in a century. The normative behavior of university-trained Ph.D.'s teaching in four-year institutions is generally not that of teachers. Faculty tend to describe the quality of their positions in terms of the number of required teaching hours under the value-laden formula of the fewer, the better. But while research (the model of preparation of college faculty) leads to basic advances in science and technology, a society that is unprepared to receive, use, and reflect on those advances will not be competitive and will not be able to create the conditions for personal growth. Teaching, not research, prepares future generations to receive, use, and reflect.

However, we continue to use the structure of graduate education as a model for undergraduate education. The result is that faculty are not liberally educated, rarely can see beyond the discipline as an end in itself, and regard the ultimate proof of their success as "original" research published in a juried journal. No matter that much of what is published in such journals is reduncant, arcane, and second-rate stuff that goes mercifully unread, it is regarded as the proper practice of the art. The more serious question is whether this type of publication—and the reward system that accompanies it—is a proper benchmark for scholarly standards. After all, we know that the core of any disciplinary research community does not depend on journal articles for scholarly communication. True advances in knowledge rarely debut in journals; rather, they appear in scholarly networks that operate in a most unsystemmatic fashion and without juries.

Mauksch (1980) has argued that the quality of postsecondary teaching is ultimately a product of the cultural and organizational environment in which it occurs. This is an attractive hypothesis, provided that it is applied as much to the graduate institution as it is to the institutions of first (and subsequent) employment. It is attractive because it poses a question as serious as that of the benchmarks of scholarly standards: Does the institutional culture value the public accessibility of teaching as it does the public judgment of research? Is it willing to place the dissemination of knowledge on a par with the advancement of knowledge? Mauksch (1980) asks us to ponder the fact that, while our research is subject to professional and public scrutiny and judgment, our teaching is not. Perhaps this is a dubious judgment on the uniquely American system of continuous assessment under which neither student nor teacher is subject to the mandatory de facto third-party evaluation inherent in external examination. Under the cloak of academic freedom, then, we too often practice mystery.

This is a complex subject, but it appears that the tensions between the disciplinary identification and institutional responsibilities of faculty have to be addressed better than they have been in the past if standards for the treatment and obligations of faculty as professionals working in an organizational context are to be maintained. I should note in this context that the percentage of college students intending to continue to graduate school in the disciplines and to pursue careers in college teaching has declined from 3.4 percent in 1966 to 0.2 percent in 1981—a frightening statistic for the future of higher education (Astin and others, 1982; Astin and others, 1967). Perhaps today's high tenure ratios have discouraged tomorrow's potential college professors. When we combine this statistic with falling scores on the GRE achievement tests in history, English, psychology, and political science and with the prevailing attitudes about the teaching role in our graduate institutions, the implications are even more frightening. When a generation of faculty retire about ten years from now, we will have little with which to replace them.

Standards of Institutional Ethics

In one sense, all our questions about standards are ethical questions. As I noted at the outset, standards refer to performance, and when we say that standards are not being met, we are referring to discrepancies between professed purposes and values—that is, intentions—on the one hand and actual behaviors (and their effects) on the other. Such discrepancies are subject to ethical judgment and warrant—nay, cry out—for resolution. Too, the language of standards is one of shoulds and oughts, of intentions and effects in human relationships; hence, in situations of conflict between values and behavior, the language of standards is a language of choice and obligation, a language of ethics.

The values of our institutions of higher learning have, in many cases, been corrupted. We can be entrepreneurial and ethical at the same time. Too often, we are not. I am not going to catalogue our sins, nor will I cite the more flagrant examples of the offering of dubious credit for courses of even more dubious quality to both traditional and nontraditional learners—principally at nontraditional sites—nor will I dwell on the ways in which colleges treat cheating and other forms of dishonesty (including deception and fraud in research) by all segments of their communities. But the recruitment of students involves institutional behaviors that are perceivable throughout the continuum of American education, and this is a form of speech that has significant influence on the expectations of students. We have been looking for bodies. What we do with minds seems to be another—and secondary—matter. The intention is in conflict with the mission of the institution, and the effects of that conflict may be devastating to individuals.

Trow (1981) has wisely observed that "important moral issues arise in this area. One can question the institution's responsibility in recruitment for what might be called 'consumer protection,' or, after students have been admitted, for providing counseling and other support services." Given what students do not know, the revolving door that results from the institution's behavior has significant ethical dimensions.

No doubt the best example of our failure to set standards for institutional conduct involves the recruitment and exploitation of student athletes. A significant number of our colleges and universities depend on both direct income from athletic programs (media contracts, gate receipts) and the indirect fund-raising and recruiting effects of those programs. For another group of institutions, the success of an athletic program is less a financial matter than it is one of institutional culture and tradition. While it would be difficult to demonstrate that colleges and universities consciously enter into given patterns of behavior toward student athletes with pecuniary ends in mind, they are imperceptibly impelled into the business of sports, and hence they are corrupted by it.

Why corrupted? Universities are presumably normative organizations performing human services designed to benefit their clients, namely students. Sports businesses are utilitarian organizations designed to benefit their owners. Start mixing the two, and a university takes on the character of the latter. Exploitation is an inevitable consequence. Given the revenues from big-time college sports, the college athlete is cheap labor coerced into an annual renewal of scholarship not by academic performance but by his or her ability to provide entertainment, revenue, and public relations to a university for forty to sixty hours a week at slave wages. The amount of education that an athlete can consume under such conditions is no more than what a college librarian, secretary, or groundskeeper who is taking classes on the side can consume. If colleges are no more inclined to provide these students with an education than the professional sports teams are to guarantee them a contract (let alone a draft) and if the system involves enticing underprepared minority students to serve in such a fashion, then we have lost our normative status in society through an abuse of power.

Accreditation: The Bottom Line

Finally—it brings a great deal of the previous explanations together—accreditation standards for postsecondary institutions are based primarily on proxy measures, not on actual student learning or on any of the other standards that I cited at the outset. This is yet another indication of our unwillingness to maintain our own stated values. Ullman (1982) likens the current state of accreditation procedures to the medical practice of triage, in which "the struggle for survival is won by those who are the fittest financially, not educationally. Those who have large endowments, generous donors, sympathetic legislatures are likely to survive. So will the superior entrepreneurs." Indeed, the practice of using proxy measures for quality inevitably leads to financial health as a criterion for continued accreditation.

Should accreditation be based on student outcomes, as was suggested to the commission on more than one occasion? Perhaps, but what outcomes, what measures, what benchmarks? If accreditation embodies the standards of a group of institutions in the same way that a license embodies the standards of a profession, then measures other than proxies are called for. But to incorporate those measures into a system that legitimizes the institutional enterprise, they must already be in place as either criteria for the credentials awarded to students or as assessments that monitor program impact and student progress.

The value-added approach to such assessments, which members of the commission discussed at a number of their panel meetings, seems to be a very attractive notion, and it has already been used on a small scale within colleges and universities. It does a great deal for the accountability of faculty and deans, and, if the feedback loop is strong enough, it does a great deal for the student's self-knowledge as well. But value added is not an easy public standard. If a student moves from ten to twenty on some measure of a given competence over four years of college, the value added may be great, but the ultimate performance is not. Another student may move from eighty to ninety. Baldly interpreted, the judgment of the value-added standard is that the performance of the first student is as good as that of the second.

For such an approach to the assessment of student progress to work, we need to agree on a reasonable threshold benchmark of performance. But assessment of institutional quality using measures of student learning does not require that benchmark. While much of our current discussion of standards for student performance focuses on the selection of measures and benchmarks — that is, on such questions as what is a reasonable threshold — we do not engage in the same discussion for institutional performance at all. Until we do, and until we include some value-added assessments of student learning among our accreditation standards, we will never play that major seventh chord for anyone.

References

Adelman, C. "Devaluation, Diffusion, and the College Connection: An Analysis of High School Transcripts, 1964-1981." Special study for the National Commission on Excellence in Education, March 1983. (ERIC document 228-244)

Astin, A. "Contradictions in American Higher Education." *Proceedings of the American Philosophical Society*, 1982, *126* (1), 6-10.

Astin, A., King, M. R., and Richardson, G. T. *The American Freshman: National Norms for Fall 1981.* Los Angeles: Cooperative Institutional Research Project, University of California at Los Angeles, 1982.

Astin, A., Panos, R. J., and Creager, J. A. *National Norms for Entering College Freshmen, Fall 1966.* Washington, D.C.: American Council on Education, 1967.

Becker, G. *Human Capital: A Theoretical and Empirical Analysis.* Princeton, N.J.: Princeton University Press, 1964.

Blackburn, R., and others. *Changing Practices in Undergraduate Education.* Berkeley, Calif.: Carnegie Foundation for the Advancement of Teaching, 1976.

Blake, H. "Demographic Change and Curriculum: New Students in Higher Education." Commissioned paper for the National Commission on Excellence in Education, August 1982.

Bowen, H. R. "Why Preserve Liberal Arts Colleges?" *Change*, 1975, *7* (9).

Hyde, W. *A New Look at Community College Access.* Denver: Education Commission of the States, 1982.

Hyman, J., Wright, C., and Reed, J. *The Enduring Effects of Education.* Chicago: University of Chicago Press, 1975.

London, H. "Academic Standards in the American Community College: Trends and Controversies." Commissioned paper for the National Commission on Excellence in Education, August 1982.

Mauksch, H. "What Are the Obstacles to Improving Quality Teaching?" Paper presented to the annual conference of the American Association for Higher Education, March 1980.

Mazzuca, L. "Admissions Standards: The Transition Process." Testimony to the National Commission on Excellence in Education, June 23, 1982.

Trow, M. "Comparative Perspectives on Access." In *Access to Higher Education*. Guildford, England: Society for Research into Higher Education, 1981.

Trow, M. "The Public and Private Lives of Higher Education." *Daedalus,* 1975, pp. 113–127.

Ullman, A. D. "Accreditation: Seal of Approval, Triage, or Cop-out." Paper presented to the Eastern Sociological Society, March 1982.

Clifford Adelman is an associate of the National Institute of Education.

*Our present virtual ignorance of the quality of
American higher education need not persist.*

Quality in the Classroom

Jonathan R. Warren

Educational quality takes a variety of forms. It can mean the quality of faculty, students, curriculum, administration, physical facilities, or of their collective product. However, at the base of most discussions of quality in higher education is a concern for the content and level of learning. Such questions as What was learned? and What levels of understanding or capability were reached? are the keys to quality. Underlying these questions is the implicit belief that certain kinds of learning and levels of understanding are appropriate to higher education and that these levels must be reached in any program of acceptable quality. For example, precollege math courses and remedial English courses produce learning that is usually not considered of college-level quality. Precollege math courses deal with content considered prerequisite to college study, while remedial English courses are designed for students whose level of accomplishment is below college standards. Decisions that distinguish what is from what is not appropriate to college study are made informally by consensus, and they can shift slowly over time. For college courses generally, quality refers to the content and level of the course material offered and the degree to which it is learned. The quality of the courses collectively is then the primary component of educational quality.

The learning of course material results from the joint activities of students and faculty. Some students learn despite occasional faculty ineptitude, and others learn despite their own minimal interest and application. However, most students learn what faculty members lay before them, and most faculty members design their courses to suit not only their own views of the content and level of material that will meet the purposes of the course, but the capabilities and inclinations of their students as well. Beyond these direct influences of student ability on what can realistically be offered and of faculty purposes on what actually is offered, the particular mix of student and faculty characteristics can also influence educational accomplishment.

Student Effects

Students' prior educational experiences and performance, general intellectual abilities, choices of fields of study or degree of uncertainty about that choice, predilections toward intellectual, social, or occupational preparation, and sociocultural backgrounds are often well known, at least in the aggregate. Some of these qualities change with educational experience as old interests are set aside, new interests develop, and academic capabilities grow, reflecting the influence of courses on students. But students also influence the courses, partly as they vote with their feet by enrolling more in some courses and fields than in others and also by responding effectively to courses at levels of difficulty they can handle while floundering in courses beyond their capabilities. Inappropriate content—for example, content that is too theoretical, too far removed from students' experiences or interests, too specialized—can also inhibit students' learning. Kerr (1982) pointed out that students make decisions about majors and courses taken, both of which influence the courses that must be offered. Students also control the total time that they spend studying and its allocation to specific courses, which influences the scope and depth of learning.

One clear illustration of student effects on what is learned is the rise over the past fifteen years in remedial courses offered in four-year colleges as the academic capabilities of the entering students declined. A national survey by the Conference Board of the Mathematical Sciences showed a 71 percent increase between 1975 and 1980 in enrollments in precollege mathematics courses in four-year colleges and universities, although total enrollments rose only 8 percent (Gardner, 1981). The effect of such courses on the learning of graduates—the intended product of the institution—is expected to be minimal. Presumably the students will remedy their mathematical deficiencies and continue their programs with only a minor delay. But the drain on the instructional resources of the institution and the disruption of students' programs as they delay taking quantitative courses impede both the students and the institution in their mutual purposes. One consequence is the development of courses that avoid quantitative requirements in fields, such as political science and psychology, where mathematical capabilities are useful but not always essential. Thus curricular offerings can be constrained by the abilities of entering students even when remedial courses are successful.

Another way in which the student effect on curriculum may have affected quality is the shift of students in recent years from liberal arts to business and engineering curricula, fields with clear occupational implications. Between 1974 and 1979, the total number of bachelor's degrees awarded declined slightly, from 946,000 to 921,000. During that period, the numbers of engineering and business degrees both grew by about 25 percent, while degrees in the arts and humanities dropped by about the same percentage. Business and engineering degrees now account for a quarter of all bachelor's degrees, while the arts and humanities make up less than 10 percent. A decade ago, the engineering and business degrees combined about equaled the arts and humanities degrees. While engineering as a field of study has oscillated over the years as the job market for engineers has fluctuated, business has shown steady growth for thirty years, and the arts and humanities have declined steadily for ten.

The changing student mix produced by growing numbers of business and engineering majors and declining numbers of humanities majors forces a change in the faculty mix as well as curricular changes. More humanities courses get designed for nonmajors, and fewer advanced humanities courses are offered. Upper-division courses like Russian Intellectual History become fewer, while courses like Urban Business Problems increase in number, and the academic climate is changed. Whether for better or worse, the nature of the collective learning of graduating students shifts as a result of changing student purposes and preferences.

The student perspective reflected in the recent shifts in field of study sees higher education in utilitarian terms, as a path toward employment and financial gain. Higher education's intrinsic value in broadening students' understanding, intellectual scope, and appreciation for the intellectual and esthetic complexities of the world is less often perceived. Similar changes have been observed in the reasons given by entering students for attending college. During the past ten years, occupational and financial reasons have become much more frequent (American Council on Education, 1972; Astin and others, 1982). Whether these changes affect the collective value of undergraduate education is a matter of personal preference, but a clear qualitative change has occurred in the product of higher education.

Except for the administrative problems associated with shifts in course demands and faculty requirements, changes produced by shifts in student choices are accepted as a necessary consequence of higher education's sensitivity to social needs. The disturbing aspect of those changes is that so little is known of their implications. For example, if business and engineering curricula were found to emphasize analytic problem-solving processes and to give little attention to integrative thinking while the arts and humanities reversed that imbalance — a distinction that is not implausible — the observed curricular shift may have produced an overall change in fundamental aspects of the product of undergraduate education. Lacking knowledge both of the general and of the many specific kinds of learning that college graduates collectively take with them, we have no opportunity to decide whether any such change in the educational product is desirable or not. That such changes do in fact occur seems incontrovertible, and an important component of educational quality is left unobserved.

Other student effects on learning need not be described in detail. The commitment of effort to studies as opposed to a part-time or full-time job, family responsibilities, social activities, or athletics affects the quality of student learning, although not always in a simple relationship. Students' interests and predilections, their responsiveness to faculty direction, and other personal characteristics clearly influence the quality of the learning that students take with them from college.

Faculty Effects

While students affect the quality of education in important ways, they do so within a context that faculty members control. Faculty members control the courses, the element that Veysey (1973) has called the most durable in American higher education. Courses are the units in which the content to be learned is organized, in which instruction occurs, and for which standards of accomplishment are set. Even the learning activities of students outside class are guided by the organization of courses. Courses successfully completed determine a student's progression through college, from lower to upper division to graduation, from introductory to advanced material, from prescribed to elective content. They provide structure to the student's major field of study. They determine how the student's general education or breadth of learning is defined. The courses taken constitute the substance of an undergraduate education.

With all the importance of courses as the building blocks of educational programs, the wide latitude that faculty members have in determining the procedures of a course and to a great extent the content as well keeps them highly variable. Variations in faculty perspective produce variations in the presentation of courses and almost certainly in the scope and depth of student learning. At present, we have no way of examining these presumed variations in student learning. If we assume, as we must, that college courses have desirable effects on the students who take them, can we also assume that any reasonable approach to a particular course is as effective as any other? In the kaleidoscopic array of available courses from which students choose about forty to constitute their undergraduate education, how do variations in faculty goals, procedures, and expectations for courses affect the educational coherence of any student's chosen forty and of the learning that they collectively represent?

The observable variability in courses and educational programs is not necessarily undesirable. A case can be made that programs are not variable enough, that faculty members in some fields are too homogeneous in their backgrounds, perspectives, and teaching objectives to provide the needed diversity. Nevertheless, under the present system, what is to be taught, how it is to be taught, the levels of student accomplishment to be sought, and the quality of the program itself are largely in the control of individual faculty members.

The central role of the course in educational programs and the high degree of autonomy that faculty members exercise in organizing and teaching their courses suggest that the views of faculty members — their perceptions of educational purposes, of subject matter structure and importance, and their expectations for student learning — are major determinants of educational success. Nevertheless, despite wide diversity and local autonomy, American higher education shows substantial coherence. With all their autonomy, faculty members respond to a variety of influences in the organization and presentation of their courses that makes similar courses in different institutions remarkably comparable — some would say too similar. All the influences originate in some way with other faculty members. The influences are then organized and filtered through formal and informal associations of faculty members and through publications by faculty members until their results are worked into the planning and presentation of individual courses.

In their early teaching years, faculty members are influenced in their choice of course structure, teaching techniques, and standards of student performance by their prior experiences as students and by other faculty members in their own department. Both these sources of influence vary with the field of study.

Textbooks are another influence on course content and procedures. This influence is probably strongest in the early teaching years, when faculty members are less sure of themselves and are teaching fairly standard introductory courses. With experience, they acquire more confidence in their own ability to give a course its structure and tend to teach more specialized courses where the selection of texts is relatively limited. While textbooks help individual faculty members to organize their courses, the relationship between textbooks and faculty members operates in both directions. Since most textbooks are written by faculty members, they serve as a vehicle for communication among faculty, reflecting to some extent the collective faculty experience with students in their courses as well as developments in the field. The influence of faculty experiences on textbook writing is biased, however, by the disproportionate number of textbook authors from a relatively few major universities (Bungum, 1980). Faculty experiences in less renowned institutions are poorly represented. Publishers reduce that bias to some extent by guiding textbook writers to produce a text that will sell in the less selective as well as in the more selective institutions, drawing their information from faculty members at large. Thus one strand in the network that maintains some consistency in higher education curricula and standards of quality despite the high level of discretion under which individual faculty members teach is provided by textbook publishers, who help a select group of faculty members write textbooks that will be useful to a broad range of faculty members in conducting their courses.

Professional journals are similar to textbooks in providing substantial direction to lower-division courses and relatively little direction to upper-division courses. In almost every academic field, one can find a journal that is devoted primarily to college teaching in that field, and some fields, such as English and physics, have several. Almost all the issues faced by college faculty members are addressed. The most notable exception is how to determine the effectiveness of instruction. Faculty members have almost no way to compare what their students have accomplished with the learning of other students in similar courses elsewhere.

The learned societies and professional associations provide reference groups, forums, and sources of authority for faculty members in the conduct of their courses. Many professional associations play a direct role in helping to determine the general content of courses offered to undergraduates, but most resist specifying content for undergraduate curricula in much detail for fear of limiting academic freedom and stifling faculty creativity. Nevertheless, some associations, through committees composed largely if not entirely of faculty members, have published recommendations that have heavily influenced undergraduate curricula and standards.

All these procedures for the exchange of information among faculty members on the conduct of undergraduate courses act to maintain some comparability among the content and even the standards for courses while allowing for diversity and exploration of new instructional approaches. Faculty effects on learning change more slowly than student effects, partly because of the faculty members' longer tenure but partly also because of the informal and even haphazard nature of the network of influences on faculty performance.

While student and faculty influences on learning and therefore on quality operate to some extent independently, they also interact (Snow and Peterson, 1980). Evidence is accumulating to indicate that some kinds of students learn more effectively with certain kinds of instructors and that some kinds of instructors are more effective with certain kinds of students that with others. For example, some students achieve more in highly structured class situations in which they are given explicit and detailed direction. Others chafe under that kind of instruction and learn better in a looser classroom environment. Faculty members also differ in their preferences for those two kinds of class situations.

Evidence of Student Learning

Clearly students' abilities and commitments of time and energy are important determinants of learning, but they are applied most effectively within a context shaped by faculty members. Knowledge of the results of that mutual undertaking of students and faculty, of the success or quality of the educational enterprise, is distressingly meager. It takes several forms, all of them inadequate, collectively as well as individually.

The most common studies of the consequences of college attendance have focused on forms of behavior that are largely peripheral to the immediate purposes of instruction. They have provided extensive information on changes in students' attitudes, preferences, and inclinations but little on increases in knowledge, understanding, or intellectual capabilities. In an exhaustive review of studies from the middle 1920s to the middle 1960s on the impact of college on students, Feldman and Newman (1969) discussed values, goals, satisfactions, attitudes, interests, and personality traits. The word *learning* does not appear in the index of their book. References to academic achievement deal with students' attitudes toward achievement and to peer and faculty influences on those attitudes. The scope and depth of the knowledge and understanding that students acquired in college were almost completely neglected.

The last fifteen years have changed the situation only to the extent that people occasionally ask why academic or intellectual development is not studied as a product of higher education. For example, Bowen (1979, p. 25) commented ruefully that "the residue of a college education—after the initial forgetting of detail—is a virtual mystery." The substantive, course-related learning toward which the resources of higher education are primarily directed continues to be neglected.

Astin (1977) summarized data from a series of longitudinal studies involving a total of more than 200,000 students in more than 300 colleges and universities. He reported changes in students' attitudes, interests, career plans, and extracurricular activities, the time-honored indicators of college effects. He also studied academic accomplishment, using grades, persistence in college, and academic honors as his indicators. Those indicators provide information on comparative levels of general achievement within single institutions. However, they give no information on what the more successful students had learned that distinguished them from students who were less successful or on what any students had learned regardless of their level of success. That information would, of course, be extremely complex, varying with field of study, institution attended, and the educational purposes and expectations of the various faculty members who assigned the students' grades. Complex as it is, however, information on what students at every level of success have accomplished in college, as well as on the maximum levels of accomplishment reached by the most successful students, is essential to any clear assessment of educational quality.

Drawing on the entire body of literature on higher education, rather than on the variables of a single though comprehensive series of studies as Astin (1977) had, Bowen (1977) found some evidence of student growth in broad intellectual skills, substantive knowledge, dispositions toward intellectual and esthetic activities, and intellectual tolerance. The broad intellectual skills were measured by verbal and quantitative tests, such as the General Test of the Graduate Record Examinations, and the substantive knowledge was measured by the GRE Subject Tests; both are limited in the information that they provide. While the broad intellectual skills and intellectual dispositions are valued by many faculty members, and are indicative of intellectual growth, they represent only minimally the objectives of most courses. The Subject Tests of the Graduate Record Examinations—content-based tests of academic achievement—are too broad and diffuse to be sensitive to the accomplishments of successful students in the more selective colleges or to the variations in accomplishment across the great variety of colleges that make up the American higher education system. They permit broad comparisons of the achievement of graduate school applicants from year to year, and institutions can use them to compare the performance of their graduates with the performance of students nationally, but comparisons such as those are not the purposes for which the tests were designed.

Changes from year to year in the achievement of graduate school applicants are interesting but difficult to interpret, primarily because the characteristics of the students taking the tests change in unknown ways as different graduate fields of study shift in their attractiveness to students. Over the past ten years, for example, graduates in mathematics, biology, chemistry, and physics have shown generally rising scores on the GRE Subject Tests. Graduates in English, history, and political science have been in a steady decline. Economics graduates declined and then recovered. After a decline in the late 1960s, psychology graduates have been stable for ten years. It is far more likely that these changes are due to shifts in the attractiveness of different fields to the current crop of college undergraduates who choose to go on to graduate school than that they are due to differences in the educational effectiveness of the undergraduate programs. The number of graduate school applicants who take the various Subject Tests change dramatically over periods of a few years, but the changes in test scores are unrelated to changes in the numbers of test takers.

Institutions examining changes in the GRE Subject Test scores of their own graduates or comparing their graduates with the most recent norms face other interpretive difficulties. The most serious difficulty is created by the diffuse nature of the content covered by the Subject Tests. Test content is determined by committees of faculty members who see that each test keeps pace with changes in the field while including content likely to have been encountered by most students majoring in the field. The number of items in a test ranges between 100 and 200; most have at least 150 items. That number of items can sample a wide range of content and provide an acceptable assessment of a student's grasp of a field in general, but not even 200 items can allow for differences in patterns of emphasis within a field. The GRE Board recognizes that limitation, as a bulletin describing the History Test (Educational Testing Service, 1982, p. 7) indicates: "The problem of content coverage in a single history test is complex. It is almost impossible to delimit the field of history in area, in time, and in scope. Moreover, no common core of knowledge is required of all history majors in all colleges."

The test is limited to United States and European history, excluding Asia and Latin America. It concentrates on political and diplomatic history, gives secondary attention to economic history, and assigns a minor role to social, cultural, and intellectual history. The questions on U.S. history refer predominantly to the period after 1800, and the majority of the questions on European history refer to the period after the Industrial Revolution. History before the Middle Ages and historical method are both neglected. The actual course patterns of history majors depart from the pattern of the test in a variety of ways, making the History Test an incomplete measure of the accomplishments of any particular history department.

For the primary purpose of the GRE, these acknowledged limitations are minor. The tests are to assist graduate schools in evaluating the preparation of applicants. Most history majors will have encountered most of the content of the history test even when their emphases have been elsewhere—on ancient history, Latin American history, or Asian history, for example. A history department that uses the GRE Subject Test to evaluate its program may find that its particular strengths and many of its upper-division courses are inadequately represented. Yet the GRE Subject Tests provide virtually the only information based on student learning now available to departments or colleges for determining the quality of the education that they offer.

Changes during recent years in tests of general academic ability, tests that are not related to the students' academic fields, have also been mixed. The General Tests of the Graduate Record Examinations have shown a fifteen-year decline in the verbal ability of college graduates who took the test but a decline and then a rise in quantitative ability over the same period. Neither test includes content taught at a level higher than high school. Instead, the tests assess verbal and numerical facility, vocabulary, reading comprehension, and reasoning. While those abilities are related to performance in college courses, they do not assess the substance of what college graduates are expected to have learned. A similar test of general intellectual ability—the Law School Admission Test—which is based heavily on verbal facility and reasoning, has shown a steady twenty-year rise.

Because other indicators of the accomplishment of departments, programs, or colleges are largely comparative, they lack substance. The most defensible indicators are the proportion of students admitted to graduate or professional schools, the proportion of students who pass licensing examinations in fields such as engineering and architecture where the bachelor's degree is the first professional degree, and the number of job offers and size of starting salaries of graduates. Graduate and professional school admissions and job offers reflect the prior experiences of schools and employers with the graduates of a department or college. Therefore, they are a realistic indicator of the quality of former graduates as judged by critical and knowledgeable observers of those graduates. The proportion of students who pass licensing examinations is more or less informative, depending on the quality and scope of the examinations and the degree to which preparation for licensure is an objective of the undergraduate program. None of these indicators gives information on what the students have learned, what their deficiencies might be, or on how a department, program, or college might raise the quality of its graduates. Moreover, all these indicators are related to the instrumental value of undergraduate education. None reflects the value inherent in an undergraduate education itself.

Grades are almost worthless as indicators of the quality of educational programs. They are entirely within the control of the faculty members in the program, and they can show high or low averages regardless of the students' actual accomplishments. Departments within a college or university sometimes find cause for pride when their average grades are lower than the grades of the same students in other departments, presumably because this indicates greater academic rigor. But those comparisons say nothing about what was learned, and it is somewhat paradoxical to base departmental satisfaction on low grades when high grades are presumed to indicate learning. A slightly informative use of average grades is in comparisons between similar departments at different institutions. If graduates with high grades from one institution perform less well in graduate school, on licensing examinations, or in employment than graduates with lower grades from the same department at another institution and if differences in student ability prior to college entrance cannot account for the differences in success, the first institution is clearly less discriminating than the second in its assessment of learning.

In summary, the only available evidence of the role that undergraduate programs play in broadening or deepening their students' intellectual capabilities—in the substance and scope of student learning—is found in the tests of the Graduate Record Examinations Board, which, because they were developed for a wholly different purpose, are not suitable for evaluating the quality of most educational programs. Attitude changes, grades, lists of academic honors, or proportions of students admitted to graduate school or to licensure do not give that information. So far as can be shown by achievement test scores, no general decline in student learning has occurred, although the average scores of people who chose to take the tests have gone up in some fields and down in others. Verbal facility and reasoning ability have declined among students taking the GRE General Tests, while they have increased among students taking the Law School Admission Test. Mathematical ability at the high school level has increased recently among college graduates taking the GRE. All this leaves us ignorant as to the quality of American higher ecucation— whether it is better or worse than it was five or ten or fifty years ago or whether it is close to accomplishing what it could if it were at peak effectiveness. We have no systematic, collective knowledge of the varied patterns of learning that occur in our colleges and universities. For example, we cannot say how history graduates differ from political science graduates or what knowledge, understandings, appreciations, or intellectual skills they are likely to have in common.

Course-Based Assessment of Learning

If the quality of higher education is to be examined in enough detail to give some sense of the scope and level of its accomplishments, better kinds of information than those now available will be needed. One such possibility is the results of course examinations. Since faculty members write their own examination questions, aggregation of these results for more than one faculty member would not be useful. However, if faculty members teaching similar courses were to collaborate, that obstacle to more broadly interpretable information would be removed, while the value of an examination to the individual faculty member would increase. For example, if two or three questions were common to the eight- or ten-question examinations of six or eight faculty members in different institutions who taught courses in which those two or three questions were pertinent, the responses to those questions could be interpreted in a broader context than that of each individual course. The collaborating faculty members would be able to compare how their own students performed on the common questions with the performance of the other groups who had been through somewhat different but pertinent learning experiences, and the examination content would still be related directly to their own course.

Different kinds of learning could be usefully aggregated at different levels. The knowledge of content, understanding of general issues, and exercise of intellectual skills associated with individual courses differ in their generality. For example, many lower-division courses in American history study the conflicting political philosophies of Hamilton and Jefferson and the partial integration effected by Madison. Knowledge of that constitutional controversy could be expected in students completing those courses in a number of institutions. Some understanding of the interplay of the political, social, and economic issues that influenced the framing of the constitution and of the processes of negotiation and compromise that allowed these issues to be resolved could be expected in students completing a broader range of courses. The ability to generalize usefully and with appropriate caution from historical events to current issues that are in some ways similar could be expected of students in still larger groups of courses. Results for each of those increasingly general kinds of learning — and others, if assessed in individual courses — could be combined across the appropriate range of courses to give detailed information about various kinds of learning.

Such a procedure would require the mutual development of examination questions, and it would work best if scoring or grading procedures were sufficiently well established that each faculty member could reliably grade the responses of his or her own students. The results could then be circulated among the collaborating faculty members. Control of the examination questions and of the results could remain with the individual faculty members, although department heads or deans might want information from a sample of courses without requiring the results to be identified with any single course.

The selection of an appropriate reference group of courses and of the kinds of knowledge or understanding to be assessed would provide evidence of educational accomplishment or quality at whatever level of aggregation was desired—all the lower-division courses in a single department at one institution, all courses of a certain kind (for example, on the American novel) at several neighboring institutions, all the courses taken by graduating seniors in a given field in a statewide university system. If the number of courses to be sampled was fairly large, fifteen or twenty questions could be inserted into different course examinations in groups of two or three. Making the questions an integral part of the course examinations would limit the cost to the cost of faculty time spent developing common examination questions for the pertinent courses. For the higher education system as a whole, the results of such assessments could be used to describe the kinds of learning produced in various fields of study, the kinds of learning attributed to general education or curricular breadth, and the variability in scope and level of learning across the system as a whole and within selected subsystems. They could also be used to answer a variety of other questions on educational quality.

The quality of American higher education is to be found in the accomplishments of students at various points within the system. Those accomplishments are organized and facilitated by individual faculty members through courses, which are the primary vehicle of instruction. A number of indicators of the learning associated with clusters of courses at different levels of inclusiveness can provide information at whatever level of scope and detail is appropriate to the purpose for which the information is to be used or to the questions that the information is to answer. These are questions that could be asked about the performance of American higher education or any of its components: What are the defacto educational standards that a department, college, or system is meeting? How stable from year to year are the educational standards? How variable is the achievement of students within any educational unit? How variable is the achievement of the educational units within a system? How adequately do current curricular offerings meet the requirements of a field in terms of scope and level of student accomplishment? How well are the general as well as specific goals of a discipline accomplished? For example, do students learn the methods of the discipline as well as its content? How well are the objects of the general education curriculum being accomplished in relation to those of the disciplines? How stable, in terms of an external reference point, are the grades assigned to students?

The quality of higher education in the United States need not remain the mystery that it has remained despite decades of study. Its accomplishments can be described in terms of a variety of indicators of the widely diversified intellectual capabilities that its graduates take with them. Components at various levels within the system can also be examined for direct indications of educational quality. Continued reliance on unsystematic impressions and inadequate indicators is indefensible.

References

American Council on Education. *The American Freshman: National Norms for Fall 1972.* Washington, D.C.: American Council on Education, 1972.

Astin, A. W., Hemond, M. K., and Richardson, G. T. *The American Freshman: National Norms for Fall 1982.* Los Angeles: University of California at Los Angeles, 1982.

Astin, A. W. *Four Critical Years: Effects of College on Beliefs, Attitudes, and Knowledge.* San Francisco: Jossey-Bass, 1977.

Bowen, H. R. *Investment in Learning: The Individual and Social Value of American Higher Education.* San Francisco: Jossey-Bass, 1977.

Bowen, H. R. "Goals, Outcomes, and Academic Evaluation." In *Evaluating Educational Quality: A Conference Summary.* Washington, D.C.: Council on Postsecondary Accreditation, 1979.

Bungum, J. L. "Institutional Domination in the Economics Profession: The Case of Textbook Writers." *Journal of Economic Education,* 1980, *12,* 51-53.

Educational Testing Service. *A Description of the History Test.* Princeton, N.J.: Educational Testing Service, 1982.

Feldman, K. A., and Newcomb, T. M. *The Impact of College on Students.* San Francisco: Jossey-Bass, 1969.

Gardner, D. P. "Quality Higher Education: A Goal for the West." *WICHE Reports,* 1981, *26* (4), 6-7, 14.

Kerr, C. "'The Uses of the University' Two Decades Later: Postscript 1982." *Change,* 1982, *14* (7), 23-31.

Snow, R. E., and Peterson, P. L. "Recognizing Differences in Student Aptitudes." In W. J. McKeachie (Ed.), *Learning, Cognition, and College Teaching.* New Directions for Teaching and Learning, no. 2. San Francisco: Jossey-Bass, 1980.

Veysey, L. "Stability and Experiment in the American Undergraduate Curriculum." In C. Kaysen (Ed.), *Content and Context: Essays on College Education.* New York: McGraw-Hill, 1973.

Jonathan R. Warren conducts research on undergraduate curricula and student learning at Educational Testing Service's Berkeley office.

Integrity of eduational standards is best served by separating the teaching and certification functions.

Examinations and Quality Control

Joseph P. O'Neill

In putting together a manual a few years ago on how to close a college in an orderly fashion, I began to notice patterns of behavior among colleges in deep trouble that might be of interest to a wider audience. My justification on focusing on institutional behavior patterns in the years just prior to an institution's closing is to outline a hypothesis that may be applicable to American higher education as a whole.

My hypothesis is this: American higher education contains structural weaknesses that are similar to a geological fault line in that the fault does not ordinarily manifest itself until the institution comes under considerable pressure. Despite the latent character of the lines of internal stress, I believe that we can begin to map their shape and direction by examining the operating practices of colleges a few years before the colleges are forced to close. As a college begins to fail, it will crack along fault lines that already exist. That is, in a vain effort to survive, an institution may begin to misuse its powers. This misuse will occur not in a random fashion but according to predictable patterns. Because patterns are not idiosyncratic to the institutions in question but represent practices generic to American higher education, the failure of one institution may mirror the internal stress lines of the enterprise as a whole.

My observations are based in part on close analysis of some thirty colleges that closed in the period between 1970 and 1979 and on a roughly equal number of institutions that are still open where steep declines in enrollment and inability to meet debt service requirements mark them as likely candidates for closure. My studies reveal how easily the basic building block of the American higher education system, the course measured in credit hours, lends itself to both financial and academic abuse.

Traditional wisdom tells us that institutions fail because they are unable to change with the times or because they are bypassed by a new technology or a new social definition of reality. Yet some of the most common characteristics of colleges that closed were a higher velocity of change, aggressive entrance into new markets, a willingness to revamp curriculum, academic year, and modes of teaching and testing in radical ways, and large shifts of students away from the liberal arts to career majors. Some of the surest signs that a small liberal arts college is in trouble are starting a weekend college, aggressive recruiting of foreign students, adopting alternative forms for granting, and establishing off-campus centers.

Those familiar with higher education finance know how lucrative an off-campus center staffed largely by part-time teachers can be. The formula for success is simple: Charge the same tuition at the outreach center as on the main campus, but pay part-time faculty only one-third of what full-time faculty receive. This enticing formula has its dangers for the small liberal arts institution. I examined the records of Ladycliff College, Milton College, and Ricker College in the years just prior to their closing and found that each had established off-campus centers in response to declining enrollment in their traditional majors: history, English, philosophy, education, and foreign languages. Unfortunately, the outreach efforts did little to increase the employment of faculty in those traditional areas. The newly recruited working adult was interested in career majors outside the competence of the regular faculty. To capture its share of the adult market, each college had to depend in large part on part-time faculty to staff the new programs in business administration, computer science, gerontology, or whatever the currently fashionable career majors seemed to be.

The result of this mismatch between existing on-campus faculty resources and the market demand off campus was that the branches foliated while the institution withered at the core. At the time all three schools closed, their off-campus business was still viable. Indeed, to satisfy creditors, Ricker sold its off-campus programs to Unity College. But the central campus could no longer pay its way.

In each instance, entering new markets or establishing new career-oriented programs were signs of weakness when the decision to initiate the change was based on a decline in enrollment in academic majors where the college's faculty resources were the strongest. To capture a share of the adult market, these colleges were forced to initiate new degree programs that were only marginally germane to their liberal arts offerings. Because they were already in a weakened financial condition, they had to depend on part-time faculty to staff the new programs and outreach centers. These new creations tended to escape the quality control procedures that full-time faculty use to safe-guard the integrity of academic programs. In their place new academic entrepreneurs arose to exploit the price-cost differential in the use of part-time faculty. These patterns of behavior are not confined to colleges that closed. In pursuit of profit, California colleges have established graduate centers in Washington, D.C., 3,000 miles away. A small Midwestern college with fewer than 1,200 on-campus students opened 154 off-campus centers, one as far away as Nome, Alaska. And one small college in New England hired an entrepreneur recruiter to package and conduct credit-bearing classes in West Virginia. The New York Times (1979) commented on this trend: "The nation's colleges and universities are traveling across the country establishing off-campus centers in a manner of an academic MacDonald's setting up hamburger facilities." And, in testimony before the House Postsecondary Education Committee, Graeme Baxter, (1979, p. 3) of the consortium of universities in the Washington metropolitan area stated: "There is growing unavoidable and embarrassing evidence that increasing numbers of institutions, particularly those struggling for survival, cannot be trusted educationally and that private accrediting bodies are neither inclined nor equipped to disapprove or to screen out those schools in a way that would protect the public interest."

Where does the fault line exist in all this? In what sense do colleges struggle for survival mirror stress lines in a much broader set of institutions? The answer lies in the self-verifying character of American higher education, both at the institutional and the faculty levels. To put it simply, there is a conflict of interest in the way in which American colleges and universities certify instruction. In the American system, there is no arms-length relationship at the undergraduate level between the teaching function and the certifying function. Faculty members not only teach but in effect guarantee, first, that their teaching meets established standards in both content and quality and, second, that students have learned what the faculty have taught. There is no external mechanism to verify the integrity of the baccalaureate degree. We are so accustomed to the conjunction of the teaching and certifying functions in individual faculty members that even the mention of separation might seem exotic. Yet, this American practice is by no means universal.

If we examine the customs of Oxford and Cambridge, we find that the colleges teach and that the university examines and certifies. An Oxford college establishes its reputation within the university by the number of firsts that its graduates receive in universitywide examinations. Tutors at Merton, Balliol, or Magdalene can take pride in their achievement because the quality of teaching and learning has been verified by a jury of peers. This same pattern of separation of powers is continued in Great Britain's polytechnics and other nonuniversity schools, where the Council of National Academic Awards not only evaluates student performance but actually grants the degrees.

The potential for the corruption of standards and the negative impact that a system based on faculty self-verification can have on the value and significance of a college degree was recognized more than a century ago by Charles W. Eliot. In his inaugural address as president of Harvard in 1869, Eliot recommended the creation of an external examining body that would be distinct from the teaching body in the granting of degrees: "When the teacher examines his class, there is no effective examination of the teacher" (Morison, 1930, pp. lxiii–lxiv).

Eliot's concerns about the role of the arm's-length examination in maintaining standards of excellence was echoed a year later by President Frieze of the University of Michigan. In his 1870 report to the regents, Frieze called the comprehensive examination "the grand leverage which maintains the scientific and literary scholarship of European universities." He said, "Take away European examinations and those noble universities would speedily degenerate or even die out. This University should endeavor to make its examinations more significant" (Smallwood, 1935, p. 28). By 1912, A. Lawrence Lowell (1912, pp. 584–585), who succeeded Eliot as president of Harvard, noted that the kind of general examination that Eliot and Frieze advocated "has now disappeared altogether, largely on account of changes brought about by the introduction of electives of some kind." Instead, he continued, the single course is "the recognized unit for purposes of examination and of counting towards the degree, which is conferred after scoring a fixed number of courses, or of semester hours made up of courses, each course being ended, closed and forever completed by its own examination."

As the distinctive American system of granting credit developed from the 1880s on, certification of knowledge took on two complementary expressions: a standard of value known as a *credit* was assigned to each course or unit of instruction, and these same credits were said to be "earned" by the learner. Assigning a certain number of credits to each course of instruction is analogous to the economic process of minting coin. Just as coining allows us to count units of precious metal rather than requiring us to weigh and assess each unit individually, making assignment of credit a way to indicate the value of instruction eliminates the need to measure the quality of each course. A three-credit course taught by a Nobel laureate and a three-credit course taught by a recently hired part-time teacher count equally toward a degree, because thirty-seven and a half hours of clock time have been spent in classroom instruction. In this self-contained course, the self-verifying faculty member not only teaches but certifies to the effectiveness of the instruction by granting credit toward a degree. Since credit is denominated by a quanity of time and since there is no external verification of the quality of instruction, colleges in hard times are tempted to choose the less expensive instructor or to pack the hall — or, in the worst of both worlds, to do both at the same time. Like governments that devalue their currency, colleges can debase the quality of instruction while maintaining the nominal credit value for courses. Large-scale use of graduate students and part-time faculty in undergraduate education has become the collegiate equivalent of clipping coin.

When the market demand for a degree is clearly distinct from the demand for instruction, the potential for corruption is obvious. Teaching is labor-intensive and inherently more expensive than certification. Institutions in financial difficulty may be tempted to use less qualified faculty where there is no external verification of the quality of their instruction. Moreover, by having the learner earn credit, colleges have used the demand for a degree to underwrite the softer market for instruction. Credit can only be got by purchasing instruction—even when that instruction is purveyed by graduate students. What market mechanism allows colleges to dilute teaching quality and still keep demand for the purchase of credit hours constant? In business, this mechanism is called a tie-in: The seller packages two distinct services so that one cannot buy the one without also buying the other. By tying credit, the more desirable product, to instruction and by offering them both at a single price—and only at a single price—colleges can maintain the demand for instruction even if it declines in quality.

However, other market mechanisms roughly measure the prestige, if not the quality, of a college's credit hour. Students who want to transfer credit from one college to another often find that they are subject to a discount rate. The credit hour becomes a medium of exchange whose conditions of transfer bear a remarkable resemblance to the world monetary system. Some credits, like certain currencies, are inconvertible except at a great discount into other credits. The acceptability of credit from one college to another gives us a rough measure of the institutional pecking order and the corresponding social stratification in American higher education.

The problems of transferability are not unique to American higher education. One of the earliest struggles in the medieval universities centered on the *ius ubique docendi*, the right to teach anywhere. Initially, this right meant that a graduate master from a prestigious university, such as Paris or Bologna, would be allowed to teach at a less well-known school without having to undergo a fresh examination of his competence. Examinations were no less distasteful in medieval times than they are today. The less well-known or newer institutions began to covet the same right. Before long, efforts were made to grant the *ius ubique docendi* by fiat. In 1233, Pope Gregory IX issued a bull extending to the graduates of the University of Toulouse the privilege of teaching at all other schools without undergoing further examination. This and subsequent bulls granting the *ius ubique docendi* rarely commanded the respect that was intended, whether they were issued by emperor or by pope. As Rashdall (1936, pp. 15–16) remarks, "the great primeval universities perhaps never recognized the Doctorates conferred by younger bodies. At Paris, even Oxford degrees failed to command incorporation without fresh examination and license, and Oxford repaid the compliment by refusing admission to Parisian Doctors, the Papal Bulls not withstanding."

Similar efforts to confer transferability of credit by fiat are not uncommon even today. Some state boards of education have regulations requiring four-year state colleges to accept without discount credit from the more recently founded community colleges, despite the fact that the older institutions dispute the parity of standards. Yet without some form of comparable exit examination, such discounting is often indistinguishable from snobbery.

The Crisis of the Faculty as a Profession

The self-contained course is the centerpiece of American higher education and in it reigns the self-verifying faculty member who teachers, examines, and certifies. The original model for this all-encompassing faculty role was the *Lehrfreiheit* of the German university professor prior to World War I. As Flexner (1930, pp. 317-318) describes him, this kind of professor "pursues his own course, unhindered. He is perfectly free in the choice of topics, in the manner of presentation, in the formation of his seminar, in his way of life. Neither the faculty nor the ministry [of education] supervises him: he has the dignity that surrounds a man who, holding an intellectual post, is under no one's orders."

In its 1915 general declaration of principles, the Association of American University Professors (AAUP) drew on the German model to describe the three elements of academic freedom: freedom of inquiry and research, freedom of teaching within the university or college, and freedom of extramural utterance and action (Hofstadter and Smith, 1968). The AAUP statement compares the appointment of a faculty member to that of a federal judge: "University teachers should be understood to be, with respect to the conclusions reached and expressed by them, no more subject to the control of trustees than are judges subject to the control of the President with respect to their decisions (Hofstadter and Smith, 1968, p. 860).

This separation of powers, unlike the separation between the teaching and certifying functions mentioned earlier, is rooted in the unique authority of knowledge, in the separation between those who know and those who do not. It is most alive in graduate education, where the pursuit of original research can mean — in fact, not just in theory — that a professor has no peers. In undergraduate education, the freedom to teach, at least as Flexner (1930) described it, is constrained by the student's need for coherence when trying to master a body of knowledge. In France, educational standards are described in a common syllabus and maintained by common examinations. In striking contrast, American colleges and schools have avoided any formal, centralized definition of the content of the baccalaureate degree. Yet in many disciplines, something resembling a nationwide consensus on course content and the sequence in which courses should be taught does seem to exist if the relative ease with which a student can transfer from one college to another is any proof.

In another chapter in this sourcebook, Warren describes the creation of an informal but powerful consensus that links individual departments at the college level with their corresponding discipline-based associations. These links in turn influence not only publishers and the materials that they produce but foundations and federal agencies in the projects that they fund. This interactive flow of information and attitude affects the way in which individual faculty members select and present course material, and it helps them to define the kinds of learning that they expect from students.

Informal standards imposed by peer pressure presuppose that individual faculty members are in direct and relatively constant contact with others in their discipline. The exchange of views in departmental meetings, the reading of papers at association conventions, and even conversation over coffee become a form of standard setting by accretion. These standards embody the culture of the profession; that is, an internalized set of behavior patterns that governs everyday conduct.

An informal system of standards begins to break down when the crucial elements of personal contact and peer pressure fail to operate. When, to maximize income or to stem losses, an institution staffs a department or an outreach center largely with those who do not share the culture of the profession, the institution's sense of its own standards erodes. London (1982, p. 15) describes the situation of the part-time teacher: "In regard to the community life of the college, part-timers rarely participate in campus activities, seldom talk with students out of class, and have virtually no contact with their colleagues ... Furthermore, they are more likely to be hired quickly and less likely to be evaluated than full-timers; in short, they are not as systematically screened. There is no data on the extent to which, if at all, standards are diluted by part-timers to curry students' favor in the hope that it will help one to be re-hired. The situation, however, is clearly one not designed to inspire faculty to adhere to high standards for their students, particularly if that makes more work for them (the faculty) while they are rushing about town, as often is the case, from one part-time job to another." In 1980, 56 percent of all community college professors were part-time instructors (London, 1982, p. 14).

This problem is not unique to community colleges. To lower the cost of instruction, many comprehensive four-year colleges, both public and private, have begun to build quotas for the employment of part-time faculty into their budget. Although these new faculty members have no opportunity to be infused with the informal standards of the discipline, they have the same self-verifying power in the classroom as do full-time faculty members. As the number of part-time teachers increases, the tendency also increases to view faculty, full-time and part-time alike, not as members of a profession who are committed to a higher code but as employees whose specific responsibilities are described in their employment contract.

Let me now tie together the first two parts of my argument. Since time is an inelastic measure, the credit hour has become a standard unit of account for most colleges and universities. Tuition is charged, degrees are awarded, and faculty are paid by the credit hour. However, if we look at this unit of account more closely, we find that it is not as uniform as it first seems. While students pay the same price for each credit hour, the cost of that credit hour to the college can vary dramatically, depending on the professor's salary and the number of students in the classroom. Time is the only constant when the credit-hour is used as a financial unit of account.

Moreover, time is a constant and a quality is a variable when the credit hour is used as the student's academic unit of account. In order to graduate, students must not only accumulate credit hours—that is, time in the classroom—they must also earn grades, and the quality of their performance in each class is measured separately. Credit hours are combined with course grades to construct a quality point index, with a minimum value required for graduation.

However, when the credit hour is used to measure faculty productivity, both time and quality are constants. The credit hours produced by faculty and consumed by students are considered to be homogeneous. No matter how well or how poorly a subject is taught, the academic credit produced by one faculty member is equal to the academic credit produced by every other faculty member when credits are counted toward a degree. To be sure, the homogenization of credit does not preclude judgments about the quality of instruction. Whether in formal evaluations or in dormitory gossip, people do distinguish between cream and skimmed milk. The system does not. And because it does not, the credit-hour system is open to exploitation, especially by an institution under financial pressure. Thus if a college staffs outreach centers or whole departments largely with part-time teachers in order to maximize income or minimize losses, then the facade of the credit hour merely masks the debasement of educational standards. At this point, the reader may ask, can accrediting agencies fill the gap in maintaining standards? That question brings me to my final point: the crisis in accreditation.

The Crisis in Accreditation

In the tradition of the dissenting churches, the power to define the substance and content of an academic degree was an exercise of both religious and social control. Until the 1870s, most colleges were an extension of the churches that founded them. In the Manual of American Colleges published in 1859, only fourteen of the 154 colleges listed were state-controlled institutions, and their share of the enrollment was only 2,508 out of a total of 18,759 (Shedd, 1932, p. 136). The American reluctance to define, much less to impose, a common content or standard of achievement for the baccalaureate degree was motivated as much by exercise of religious freedom as it was by academic freedom. State legislatures granted college charters and full authority to confer degrees with few or no strings attached.

In contrast, European nations, responding to a different set of religious issues, moved toward centralized control. For example, in the reform of French higher education after the Franco-Prussian War, a secular state diluted the role of the church in education by a peculiar definition of academic freedom: "Liberty was proclaimed for higher education: any group whatever could open a college. But the state would retain the granting of degrees" through a system of state examinations (Bougle, 1932, p. 27). Although they were in no way controlled, Oxford and Cambridge defined the content and standards for the degree through universitywide examinations. Only in the American system is the degree defined incrementally by each course that a student takes. Common to both the Oxford-Cambridge system and the French system of state examinations is a drive toward epistemological "realism"; that is, an effort to make the degree carry some closely defined meaning across a large number of students. In comparison, the American approach is a form of nominalism in which baccalaureate degrees from different institutions can represent very different kinds of intellectual achievement.

The American system of accreditation has responded to this de facto nominalism in defining the content and standards for the award of degrees with an artful ambiguity of its own. As Millard explains in another chapter in this sourcebook, the regional accrediting associations have tended since the early 1930s to use a mission-objective model in defining educational standards. Each college defines its own educational objectives. Then it is judged on how well it meets the goals that it has set for itself. If the mission-objective model is pushed to its logical extremes, it might seem pure relativism. But in practice, informal prescriptive standards—never, of course, closely defined—set boundaries to the meaning of college-level work. Since regional accrediting agencies do not examine students to determine the quality of instruction—requiring such an examination would in itself be an unacceptable act of control—accreditors infer the quality of an educational program indirectly. Some inferences can be based on output measures, such as the number of students placed in graduate or professional schools, but most of the accreditation process focuses on a measurement of inputs, that is, on how many faculty members hold the doctorate in their discipline, on articulation in the curriculum, and on the adequacy of laboratories and library holdings in terms of institutional mission. Any inference drawn from inputs, whether they be faculty, library, or facilities, is inherently less convincing that an inference drawn from outputs, such as student performance. Output evaluation is similar to the bubble chamber in physics. Even if the interaction cannot be seen, the observer can at least measure the trail that it leaves.

The current crisis in accreditation lies in the unwillingness or inability of higher education to define minimum standards. The National Commission on Excellence in Education concentrated on admissions standards. At least four states—Georgia, Florida, Texas, and New Jersey—have under discussion statewide examinations for the transition between the sophomore and junior years of college. Implicit in this movement is a form of accreditation more akin to the European system of defining outcomes and then testing to see whether they have been met.

If American higher education is to forestall the imposition of a state system of examinations, it will have to improve its own forms of quality control.

Neither evaluation of inputs by the accrediting associations nor the integrity of faculty placed in an inherent conflict of interest can be fully relied on in a severe financial crunch. If the academy does not strengthen these controls of its own volition, it may find government moving to do so in ways that jeopardize the core of the enterprise.

The most convincing way to improve the integrity of our educational standards is to establish at the institutional level an arms-length relationship between the teaching and certifying functions through comprehensive examinations. Such examinations could be formulated by the faculty of an entire department or school. Where the department was made up of one or two members, as it often is in small colleges, the Graduate Record Examination or some other standardized test could be used.

I do not mean to imply that the European regimen of state examinations or even the English system of universitywide examinations is without fault. Adam Smith (cited by Hutchison, 1978, p. 23) once remarked that, had the universities of Oxford and Cambridge gained a monopoly on the education of doctors, "the price of feeling a pulse might by this time have risen from two or three guineas, the price at which it has now happily arrived, to double or treble that sum, and English physicians might have and probably would have been the most ignorant and quackish in the world."

In his study of the development of the French universities from the Second Empire to the Great War, Weisz (1983, p. 216) pointed out that one examination, the *agregation* in the faculty of letters, continued to be a barrier to research until well into the 20th century. Newman (1982, pp. 109–110) remarked that if he had to choose between a University that dispensed with residence requirements and awarded degrees merely on the basis of examinations and "a University which had no professors or examinations at all, but merely brought a number of young men together for three or four years," he would choose the latter.

Yet examinations are also the ordinary vehicle of reform. A new system of examinations helped to rouse Oxford and Cambridge from their late-18th-century torpor and to make Newman's Oxford a far different place than Adam Smith knew only a generation before. In the reform of American medical education at the beginning of this century, the licensure examination became the keystone in the American Medical Association's efforts to close down inadequate medical schools. The question facing American higher education is whether control of examinations will rest with the state or with individual institutions.

In the swing of the pendulum between the faculty member's freedom to teach and the system's need to verify the integrity of its standards, we have moved too far from quality control. At a time when financial crises can so easily erode institutional integrity, reinstitution of the comprehensive examination would send a positive signal to society at large that our colleges and universities are not foundering.

References

Baxter, G. Quoted in *Higher Education and National Affairs,* 1979, *28* (19).
Bougle, C. "The French Conception of the University." In *The University in a Changing World: A Symposium.* Oxford: Clarendon Press, 1932.
Flexner, A. *Universities: American, English, German.* New York: Oxford University Press, 1930.
Hofstadter, R., and Smith, W. (Eds.). *American Higher Education: A Documentary History.* Chicago: University of Chicago Press, 1968.
Hutchison, T. W. *On Revolutions and Progress in Economic Knowledge.* Cambridge: Cambridge University Press, 1978.
London, H. "Academic Standards in the American Community College: Trends and Controversies." Commissioned paper for the National Commission on Excellence in Education, July 1982.
Lowell, A. L. "Examination of Subjects Instead of by Courses." *Harvard Graduate Magazine,* 1912, *20* (30), 584-585.
Morison, S. E. *The Development of Harvard University Since the Inauguration of President Eliot 1869-1929.* Cambridge, Mass.: Harvard University Press, 1930.
The New York Times, January 7, 1979.
Newman, J. H. *The Idea of a University.* Notre Dame, Ind.: University of Notre Dame Press, 1983.
Rashdall, H. *The Universities of the Middle Ages.* Oxford: Clarendon Press, 1936.
Shedd, C. "Higher Education in the United States." In *The University in a Changing World: A Symposium.* Oxford: Clarendon Press, 1932.
Smallwood, M. L. *An Historical Study of Examinations and Grading Systems in Early American Universities.* Cambridge, Mass.: Harvard University Press, 1935.
Weisz, G. *The Emergence of Modern Universities in France, 1863-1914.* Princeton, N.J.: Princeton University Press, 1983.

Joseph P. O'Neill is executive director of the Conference of Small Private Colleges, Princeton, New Jersey.

Quality may well require standards that are institution-specific.

The Administrator's Role in Providing Educational Excellence

Thomas J. Hegarty

The foremost concern of an academic administrator at a college or university with regard to the advancement of educational excellence is to provide well-prepared, student-oriented, intellectually active faculty members who develop and teach exciting and well-conceived programs and courses to selected young people who can benefit from the experience. In the process, the administrator must keep four things uppermost in mind: the institution's mission, society's needs, and the appropriateness of the mix of the university's programs; the regular evaluation of programs and courses; the full development of existing faculty talent and the careful recruitment of faculty replacements; and the maintenance of a student recruitment policy that encourages enrollment by students who are prepared to participate in what the institution has to offer. The administrator must also work to develop strong academic support services in four areas: a library that fully supports the teaching mission and that provides at least the beginning stages of support for student and faculty research; a computing center that permits both faculty and students to become fluent with computers and that supports the programs and professors who are already making effective use of the computer for teaching, learning, and research; a media center to encourage various styles of instruction and learning; and an advising system that, wherever possible, arranges for faculty members to help students make wise choices of courses and programs, services and careers.

J. R. Warren (Ed.). *Meeting the New Demand for Standards.* New Directions for Higher Education, no. 43. San Francisco: Jossey-Bass, September 1983.

The most useful tool for administrators in meeting their obligations is information from evaluations, whether done formally or informally and whether launched individually or as part of a general accreditation or state review process. The university has been amazingly responsive over time to the demands of state, society, and individual, but it also needs autonomy to carry out its role. It needs some distancing from its critics, and it needs some time to consider the validity of the advice offered. The university does not need to abdicate its responsibilities for what is offered and for how it is offered to an accrediting association, professional group, state government, or federal agency, although these sources can provide some useful advice. Fortunately, in the American tradition, there are comparatively few people or offices external to colleges and universities that want to take on the universities' job. Where voices are raised to take decision making out of the universities, I reply that compelling arguments from outside the university have always made themselves felt—in our market- and consumer-centered higher education system, the university that fails to heed its mission and duties will be sharply reminded of the fact—and that universities, in the United States as elsewhere, serve more than current students. Among their numerous clienteles are former students, future students, and learning itself; that is, the tradition of transmission of and addition to knowledge. All colleges and universities have these clients, although their responses to them are different.

I applaud Warren's question, How do we know that quality is down? The answer is, of course, that we do not know that quality is down. Academic administrators, especially academic deans, who are the most active institutional aggregators and users of appropriate information, realize that we have only impressions of how students are actually performing. We do often receive complaints from faculty on the low caliber of entering students or on how students are progressing. Unfortunately, many of us have heard the same complaints, under differing conditions of growth or decline, for the last thirty years. I sympathize with the observations of decline and believe that entering students do not read as quickly or as reflectively as earlier generations of their peers. Knowing the role of television and computers in young people's educational development, I can understand the decline in reading. But I also wonder what new kinds of knowledge students now bring to the university as a result of their experiences. How have we used it, and have we challenged it? We do not know, and we should.

Warren's concern that quality cannot be addressed effectively until educational purposes are clear is well based. So, too, is his statement that we have not been successful in measuring the degree to which educational purposes are being accomplished in students. Academic administrators need to know how to build on our faculty's unique observations of students, for they alone know what is actually happening in their classrooms. But in order to help faculty focus on the appropriate detail, we must help them learn to be observers and perceivers.

Indeed, the rise and fall of faculty perceptions would be a most useful measure of changes in educational quality within an institution. However, I see little reason to aggregate the data beyond the institutional level. The changes in which we are interested occur on one campus at a time. The glare of publicity or odious comparison could retard both continued observation and corrective or enhancing action. Moreover, I prefer the narrative approach over quantification, if only because it is the one with which faculty members are generally more comfortable. Quantifying is useful if one is going far beyond an institution's wall or if one is addressing researchers in higher education. It is not helpful to typical faculty members, who inevitably will be asked to make changes if decline or weaknesses are observed. Narrative will satisfy Warren's insistence that the information be clear enough to be understood by someone who was not present when the events or occurrences described took place. Incidentally, most administrators would welcome help from the Educational Testing Service or from regional accrediting bodies, a federal panel, or the state boards of higher education in developing easily applied methods that would enable them and their teaching colleagues to study and catalog change on their own campus. The role of suggesting and guiding campus change is appropriate for the external bodies. The role of analyzing numbers and issuing general prescriptions is not.

Accreditation

Millard is helpful in Chapter One by pointing out that the accreditation process does not pretend to determine institutional or program quality. He correctly asserts that only institutions and programs can do that. He does show, however, the crucial role that accreditation plays in assessing whether an institution or program is carrying out its commitment to quality and providing incentives to enhance it. I concur with him that accreditation is the primary communal self-regulatory means.

After a review of the history of accreditation, which is helpful even to the reader who is generally aware of the growth of the process, Millard discusses the evolution of standards of quality. He describes the earliest definitional-prescriptive model and its gradual replacement by the mission objective model. He shows how a program-professional model for specialized programs has emerged alongside to provide coverage for fields where universities have increasingly been asked to share responsibility with outside professional associations. He may be correct that the expansion of specialized accreditation bodies is not proliferation, but academic institutions all too often feel the pressure of too many uncoordinated visits by separate accrediting teams. The solution may be not in limiting the number of accrediting bodies but in improving the coordination of their services and in giving more recognition to the rights and duties of individual institutions. Millard suggests that increased competition for students may cause some institutions to lower standards and to add ill conceived and poorly integrated off-campus programs. By now, the lesson taught by closures of overextended institutions should keep others from following their example. We may well see a new reaction of belt tightening and close attention to institutional fortes and less academic adventurism. Millard's four definitions of quality are thoughtful and thought-provoking, as are his explanations of standards, criteria, and indexes. Of the definitions of quality, the fourth, achievement in kind, which is related to institution or program objectives, as well as some aspects of the second definition, social consensus, seems the most useful to those who administer institutions.

I differ on one important point with Millard. Quality may well require standards that are institution-specific if each of our 3,300 colleges and universities is to grow in distinctiveness. For whose benefit must everything be nationally generalizable? Accrediting agencies have not changed bad institutions or enhanced good ones through the emphasis on generalities. Colleges and universities ought to be encouraged to become all that they can be, each according to its own model. Typologies will emerge, but by the end of the eighties, they may be rather different from those that we have already seen. Moreover, Millard's desire to look at students' reasons for coming to a certain institution may not yield much by itself. Surely, a more useful approach would be to look at institutional goals and programs and the success with which they are communicated to prospective or actual students. In my mind, an institution has the obligation not just to respond to students' ideas on education or career but positively to guide their development in both areas. Fortunately, students' ideas are continually changing. At what point in their evolution can institutions be judged by their preferences?

I wholeheartedly agree with Millard that reputation alone tells us little about an institution's current success. Of course, resources relate to success; processes and outcomes are both important. I applaud the desire to set standards relative to objectives. Finally, I consider Millard's section on the effective use of accreditation to be required reading both for team members from regional associations as well as for the officers and faculty of the campuses that are visited.

State Policy

I was disappointed by Chapter Two, which reviews the legal responsibility of states for education. The question is not easy to study, because the powers of the various state agencies differ considerably. As a campus officer, I have heard many horror stories from colleagues about state board–directed planning exercises of a five- or ten-year frame that yielded no tangible results, about program reviews that ended up in the courts, and about program approval processes that delayed action on much-needed programs until the need had passed. Whatever the desires of the officers and staff of state boards may be in this regard, it is clear that the American system of higher education has provided the states with only a modest role for direction. Independent institutions are normally all but exempt from their control, and public institutions often launch or continue programs without authorization. Would it not be more useful to the development of a coherent plan in education if state boards were to take on the function of analyzing statewide trends that would help to guide not only institutions but students and parents in making the wisest choice of program and prospective career? Boards and board staff might even lead the discussion about apparent changes and their significance. In the free market of higher education, information is a tremendous source of power. It can help to close bad institutions and to enhance the position of good institutions. It can cause new programs to be established and unnecessary ones to be phased out.

Let me add a personal note here: when state agency representatives visit campuses for program review, they should be encouraged to join other accrediting groups so that the visit is less disruptive to the proper business of higher education. Where possible, the state board might do better to contract its program review duties out so as not to have to maintain a large staff in a time of fiscal stringency or overwork a small one to cover the spectrum of academic programming. The distinction made between the concerns of regional accrediting groups and state boards seems to be artificial: Any good accrediting team now looks at resource allocation, access, consumer protection, and productivity. I repeat here my strongly felt belief that real change and improvement occur on a campus that is well fortified with useful information: No state board or staff, regardless of the talent found within it, can by itself create quality education. Some means of delimiting the task of the state agency and of helping it to work hand in hand with institutional faculties and administrators can improve the climate for higher education within state boundaries.

Standards

In Chapter Three, I benefited from Adelman's clear distinction between requirements and standards as well as from his several approaches to standards. In general, however, his chapter seems to be devoted to presenting some worst-case observations about American higher education. Not all institutions are violating standards of content, nor have considerations of the process of learning impaired course design; many courses are distinctly better as a result of the effort. The decline in GRE scores is a matter that still requires study, as is the corresponding increase in scores by college graduates on the law boards. Faculty members and college administrators, who—despite Adelman's claim—do not always run the show, do try to refer to student learning wherever possible. Faculty members often make assessments that they share in departmental meetings and sessions of committees of the faculty senate and administrators often receive reports. However, until administrators can convince faculty members that information on poorly performing students will not be used against them when they are assessed as teachers, faculty may prefer to complain without significant written follow-through.

Whatever one thinks of raising SAT cutoff scores to ensure an influx of better students, the action does indicate that colleges and universities are beginning to become aware that no institution can serve every constituency equally well and that some effort must be made to identify and admit students who can benefit from the institution's offerings. The separation of institutions by function needs to be studied by good minds. It might be a suitable task for the National Institute of Education or for the follow-up group to the National Commission on Excellence in Education.

I agree with Adelman and O'Neill that use of the college credit and allocated time as a proxy for learning is unfortunate. However, I must also ask what other measure would permit students to transfer from one institution to another? It is not the college credit system that has failed as an accounting mechanism. Rather, faculty and administrators at many institutions have failed to help prospective and actual students to free themselves from the mean and cynical view that a college education is the amassing of a number of credits. Most universities are working on this problem. The recurrent interest in general education, whether through a core curriculum or an improved distribution system, is manifest proof that educators are aware that undergraduate (or, for that matter, graduate) education is more than the accumulation of courses and credits.

I do not understand Adelman's attack on vocational, preprofessional, and career curricula. The liberal arts and sciences are not at war with career or professional education. The two kinds of education, which are different, are also quite complementary. In recent years, a number of professional fields have been taught at the most distinguished liberal arts colleges, in ways that emphasized their theoretical nature. From that point of view, these professional fields have been co-opted into the liberal arts or the sciences. Not all courses are equally useful to the development of students' minds, but neither do all courses allow students to complete the undergraduate or graduate degree. If the complaint is that some universities offer inappropriate courses, my question must be, inappropriate to whom and for what purpose? Until I know that, I would prefer to suspend judgment. The argument that diversity is better served by the number of sites that a university maintains and by the time of day at which courses and programs are offered, not by the diversity of offerings, is to beg the point. There are students who want and need career programs, and there are institutions whose missions permit them to offer career programs. The better institutions insist that their students also choose courses in the liberal arts and sciences, despite the nature of the major field. After all, can everyone become an English or history major? Indeed, should they? Some institutions, including by own, make generous use of the concept of double majors to permit students to receive preprofessional or career training and a sold basis in the liberal arts.

The real question that we all must ponder is, How should the curriculum change so that it can address the knowledge explosion and the changed needs of our economy and society? Students clearly need to learn that we depend on science and technology, that we are now living in a global village, and that this is a multiracial and multicultural society. Our institutions also need to respond to the changing composition of most student bodies to include more women and more nontraditional students, especially ethnic minorities and older adults.

Regarding standards of communication, I heartily agree with Adelman that we have not always done a good job in communicating institutional processes and expectations for academic work to students. I do not agree that students are seeking an identity through the major. In the last decade, students have seemed to come in with at least a tentative career or job in mind. The major is a means of advancing toward career goals. But it is also an important building block in the undergraduate curriculum, permitting depth and balance to the general education component and to the student's use of electives. Student identity comes from the student's sense of participation in a community of learning. In this outcome, the extracurriculum of the university plays a significant role — whether in the fraternity, sorority, residence hall, student union, athletic team, or cultural group — in building the student's sense of community and involvement.

No one now questions that institutions must be honest in advertising what they have to offer, as well as in the more detailed communications that they share with their students. The era of untrammeled entrepreneurism in education may in fact have passed, even as a swelling chorus of voices now denounces it. Certainly, on the issue of exploitation of student athletes, we see major efforts being made by colleges and universities on the one hand and by professional associations on the other to avoid, and where necessary to correct, abuses. I might mention, however, that the expenditure of funds on athletics, including football, does not necessarily mean that institutional resources are being squandered. Athletics is an important factor in the retention of those who participate, and often the presence of good teams and opportunities to observe first-class college competitions retain students who are not personally active. Not all institutions have been corrupted by athletics, nor are they all in the sports business.

Administrators want to look at measures of change in students as a result of college and university learning. However, they have learned from experiments with the value-added approach that it is hard to separate the effects of four years of maturation, outside employment, and the impact of new, more adult relationships from educational effects. Until some of the good minds that now criticize colleges and universities help to refine the techniques, can any of us really look at the value-added effects of college on student learning?

Quality

Chapter Four—Warren's chapter on quality in the classroom—is a major contribution to an understanding not only of our ignorance about the academic aspects of American higher education but also of ways in which faculty and administrators can learn more about what is going on at their college or university. Warren is correct in saying that what is acceptable for college credit changes informally by consensus over time. Many institutions today permit credit for experience that in the past would have been taken for required noncredit "enrichment." The effect on the curriculum of the lower reading ability and the lessened mathematical prowess of many students is considerable. Not only are introductory offerings changed, but the content of later courses, or courses in other disciplines that might be taken in the freshman and sophomore year, have been adjusted downward to reflect the students' average level. This effect on the content of learning needs to be assessed carefully by each university faculty. Warren is also right that students' changes in fields of interest have affected the curriculum. Many universities have struck back by encouraging second majors or academic minors or clusters of programs that will serve to make the undergraduate experience more balanced and complete. In hiring faculty educational administrators are aware of the growing numbers of students in such areas as business, engineering, and computer science, as well as in some of the health and social service fields and of the need to provide more faculty, often at the expense of positions in the liberal arts and sciences. Perhaps fewer advanced humanities courses are being offered now than twenty years ago. However, do we know the real impact of this change? From one point of view, bringing students in to programs in engineering or business means turning them over for large percentages of their course work to the humanists, the social scientists, and the natural scientists. Are not more introductory humanities courses being taught? Moreover, can we really say that skills are taught only in traditional liberal arts courses? For example, can analysis be taught as well in business or in engineering as it is in chemistry or in philosophy? I do not know, and I suspect that few people do. This may be a fruitful area of research: What skills are in fact fostered by what academic areas? If we discover that different major areas emphasize different skills, then should we not tailor our general education programs to complement and supplement what is being learned in the major? If second majors permit the development of complementary skills, should this not become a standard approach to advising a career-minded student?

Sadly, Warren is also right that the one professional issue not faced in the disciplinary journals is how to help a faculty member determine the effectiveness of his or her instruction. This being the case, would it not be a useful subject for the Educational Testing Service, or state boards, or a national commission to pursue? There are interested academic administrators as well as faculty members who will assist in carrying out well-conceived plans. The recent experiment by the American Association of State Colleges and Universities in its Academic Program Evaluation Project shows that faculty members want to know how well students are learning in their classes and will help devise campus-specific instruments for checking mastery of both content and skills.

Warren's proposal for course-based assessment of learning is a step forward in coming to grips with measuring student learning. While I approve, I suggest that attempts to aggregate information at levels beyond the campus will prove cumbersome. Why not instruct the institutions in how best to observe learning in their students and ask those institutions to establish and defend their own norms? Real change will be institution-specific. No test or outside agency can accomplish what the faculty and administration can carry out within their own walls. The thoughtful questions with which Warren concludes represent the first solid approach I have seen to the assessment of changing performance in American higher education. The questions are answerable, however, only on an institution-specific basis.

Quality Control

I have serious problems with Chapter Five. On the simplest level, O'Neill seems to blame American higher education for not having followed the European model. Why should it have? Higher education in Europe has been far less successful than higher education in America. Moreover, I do not believe that the great culprit in the American higher education system is the credit hour. I do agree with O'Neill that sudden changes in institutional style have often foreshadowed the collapse of colleges and universities. In particular, every academic administrator is aware of the lucrative nature—and pernicious effect—of an overextended off-campus program. There is no academic administrator who has not been cautioned to help his institution stick to its strengths. In fact, the current wisdom in academic administration is that no institution should attempt to deliver all services to every group. Instead, it should develop its own mix and position itself where it can draw on its faculty and service strengths as well as on societal needs and interests. I doubt, too, that separating the certifying function from the teaching function would solve some of the problems in higher education. The certification of teachers for the primary and secondary schools is generally a function of a state agency, yet it has not spared teacher education from serious problems and from more strident criticisms.

Because O'Neill devotes so much attention to academic credit, it seems well to remind him that institutions can decide what they will accept as transfer credit and, more specifically, that they can rule out courses that do not fit their own patterns for general education, majors, or minors. We often see students graduating with superfluous credits but barely satisfying the content requirements of their final institution. I recognize that in many state systems, faculty and administrators are concerned that community college credits may often be forced on a receiving four-year college or university by a statewide compact. The result has been that senior college faculty have begun to work jointly with community college faculty to design courses helpful to students who plan to transfer.

The use of part-time faculty is in some institutions less than perfect, but the better colleges and universities are concerned about socializing part-timers, especially those hired on a regular basis, into the operation of departments and schools. Moreover, institutions have discovered that they can enhance their curricula by the choice of excellent full-time professionals as part-time instructors. While their services are often not cheap, these people bring not only fresh points of view to the academic classroom but connections with the world of work. If O'Neill is unhappy with the credit hour and the quality point index, he should try to help his peers develop a new and better way. The frequent review of grading policies and allotment of credit hours on each campus provides ample proof that there is little complacency about current practice. However, until a better system is devised, few institutions will be able to stray from what O'Neill dislikes.

A few years ago, the Carnegie Commission expressed fear that American institutions of higher education were becoming remarkably similar. In contrast, O'Neill seems to be concerned that there is too much diversity. It is not the job of accrediting agencies to make our colleges and universities more alike but rather to help each one, within its chosen mission, become all that it is capable of being. I do not agree that the current crisis in accreditation lies in higher education's unwillingness or inability to define minimum standards, and I hope that the four states mentioned will not follow through with their ill-advised discussion of statewide examinations of college students in the transition between the sophomore and junior years. What will they test? How relevant will the test be to specific institutional curricula? Who will design it? The fact that such testing is akin to the European system is scant comfort to me.

I support O'Neill's recommendation for comprehensive examinations, since they would help departments and schools within a university come to grips with the totality of student learning across their curricula. The spring semester of the senior year is now at many institutions an academic and intellectual wasteland, as students who have finished their course work and received early grades wait for graduation to occur. This time could well be used for comprehensive examinations that could do much to help students, faculty members, and administrators understand exactly what has been learned in four years at the institution. The results of such comprehensives could go far toward causing faculty mavericks to reassess what they do with class time. Such subtle pressure, institution by institution, seems likely to be more successful than any effort to design national curricula or continentwide testing.

Integrity

Integrity, which can be defined as an institution's doing what it says it will do, is ultimately the means of ensuring quality in higher education. Integrity requires faculty and administrators to watch over the process, and it means that students must take some responsibility for their own learning. It implies that faculty members keep in touch with changes in their own discipline, among their own students, and across their own campus. It requires administrators to follow up throughtfully on information provided by external and internal sources and to advance the debate on the nature and purpose of undergraduate and graduate education. Everyone on a campus needs to come to grips with the many purposes of education. Everyone needs to realize that preparation through the major of apprentice scholars in the liberal arts or sciences or of preprofessionals in the professional programs cannot be the only goal. From that realization will flow improvements in the teaching of courses and in the assignment of course credit for various experiences and refurbishment of the institution's general education program, which may have to be tailored to the needs of constituencies that differ in age, preparation, and choice of major program. The faculty and the administration have joint responsibility for the coherence of the curriculum; no group can afford to be concerned only about its own specialty. Administrators need to put themselves more often in the position of teaching faculty, offering course work where possible. Faculty immersed in one discipline need to refer in class to the courses of other disciplines. Across the university, everyone has responsibility for improving the writing and speaking skills of students as well as for encouraging their powers of analysis, synthesis, and quantification. Everyone also needs to give attention to the values implications of university activities as well as to the subject matter of courses so that students can develop and enhance their own value systems and recognize and come to tolerate the value systems of others.

Ultimately, universities need some freedom from knee-jerk criticisms as well as some distancing from external inquisitors. The job of building or enhancing quality education and effective student learning will be done on individual campuses. Professional accrediting organizations can help by continuing to respect universities' efforts to be distinctive in settings and carrying out their goals. State boards can help by bringing to every campus increased information about student numbers, student interests, career opportunities, and societal and economic changes. Where they contribute to an assessment of programs, they can share the information fully and nonpunitively with campus leaders. Where they recommend program phaseout, they should give the campus an opportunity to shift resources to improve and retain a program that it views as necessary. State boards can deal efficiently with requests for new programs, granting or denying them in such a way that the would-be clientele does not go away in exasperation. The coming of out-of-state programs to certain parts of the country has often been the direct result of the failure of institutions or of state boards to respond to the needs of the local citizens. Finally, bodies like the National Commission on Excellence in Education can help to identify questions needing research and use the experts who appear before them to develop methods that can be translated into procedures, campus by campus, among American colleges and universities. The universities can then heal themselves and strive more effectively toward excellence. That, I believe, is everyone's goal.

Thomas J. Hegarty is vice-president for academic affairs at Butler University in Indianapolis.

The demand for quality can become an opportunity for administrators to foster renewal and new directions in their institutions.

What Can Administrators Learn from this Sourcebook?

Frederic M. Hudson

What can administrators learn from the chapters in this sourcebook? How can we improve our management strategies around issues of standards, quality, and accountability? How can we, as administrators, affect educational excellence?

First, the chapters suggest that there is not much agreement on how to define educational quality. I think that we should be glad. During the past decade, we have witnessed heated debate over quality assurance and control in higher education based on industrial production experience. The debate has invariably been dominated by concern for responsible management of diminishing financial resources within higher education. From a broad perspective, the quality debate is about educational decline and depression. After a quarter-century of enormous growth, prestige, and intrinsic authority, institutions of higher education are entering a decade with declining enrollments, an undercurrent of negative social attitudes toward higher education, economic roller coasters, and rapidly changing student demographic characteristics.

In such a scenario, where do the cries for standards, quality, and accountability come from? They come from two sources: from those within the establishment of higher education who want to sustain the glorious days of the past, creatively or demonically; and from those outside higher education who want us to serve external interest groups—accrediting commissions, postsecondary state agencies, professional organizations, licensing groups, industry, and political forces. While administrators must know the legitimate concerns of the internal and external forces, the debate over quality needs to be a philosophical debate of a larger order. At stake in the ongoing furor over quality assurance and control are the fundamental purposes and goals of our various university systems. The basic beliefs of our institutions ought to shape the priorities of our educational decisions. Educational excellence should mean *this* for *this* school with *these* goals and *these* priorities. Ours is a philosophical task—to help institutions sort out their values and beliefs in a society that is struggling with its own sense of purpose. I am suggesting that we have an opportunity to change the nature of the quality debate. By keeping the focus on the renewal of our various institutions, we can determine for ourselves both how to reform our limited resources and how to address the concerns of social agencies.

Administrators play a key role in the maintenance of excellence in academe. More than any other group inside or outside their school, administrators are sensitive to the various issues and groups within their institution. They must also be sensitive to the political, social, and economic forces surrounding their institution. Perhaps more than in previous eras, administrators have an opportunity to be midwives, brokers, and consensus builders. The clamor for quality can be an opportunity for institution building.

If we center the quality debate on the belief systems and unique purposes of our institutions, the meaning of quality will have to be broad and philosophical. Education, by definition, deals with ethical and esthetic values, personal development, intellectual refinement, professional issues, and life-long learning. Each school treats these issues differently. Within our institutions, students and teachers are involved in moral issues, citizenship, self-awareness, communication skills, esthetic sensibilities, professional development, and intellectual articulation. Whatever quality and excellence mean must be found in the processes through which these issues are pursued. Those processes are likely to be pluralistic and complicated, not uniform and regimented.

University administrators seldom begin with a neat definition of educational excellence that they then apply to their situation. Rather, they typically foster, then implement contextual concepts of quality assurance within the institutions they administer. Millard's fourth, contextual definition of educational quality is the best normative point of departure for developing an administrative strategy. Administrators begin any educational assessment with working definitions of quality that function within the particular educational situations in which they work. Talk about educational quality is tentative, situational, contextual, and relative. Educational excellence is pluralistic, and any attempt to validate our standards is bound to please some and displease others.

The meaning of quality in our institutions comes from legitimate conflict among the self-interests of the members of academe. Teachers are especially interested in instructional quality, while students are more interested in learning. Vocationally oriented professionals look for competence-based qualities, while liberal arts professors are more concerned with intellectual achievement. The board may concentrate on financial management issues. Quality is not the province of any one group in the education process; rather, it is the product of the legitimate conflict of the various members of a school. The administrator has the task of keeping this conflict fair and creative. Administrators need to foster open debate among the various factions that have a self-interest in the priorities of our institutions.

Regarding this definition of quality for our own institution, our primary responsibility as administrators is to get our institution to be clear about the intrinsic, limited, and particular quality issues that apply in our particular educational setting. We can be proud of both our differences and our similarities. We each have different geographies, clienteles, value orientations, curricular emphases, degree programs, institutional pressures, and financial capabilities. We also have the same general mandate—to educate—and that should be a basis for providing society with some assurance of quality having to do with learning, teaching, and administering. As administrators, we have the opportunity and the responsibility to define the parameters of quality issues and to develop self-responsibility for ascertaining quality within our institutions in a way that communicates clearly with members of our society.

Second, if administrators choose to evolve quality issues from within their own institution, how can they establish quality assurance that can be demonstrated with some objectivity? How should administrators deal with outside pressures for standards, accountability, and accreditation? Sometime in the mid-sixties, education lost its mystique for Americans at large. Since then, we have been defending our rights and privileges against an external audience that doubts us. The locus of control for the quality debate is currently outside our institutions, pressing themes of vocational relevance, professional standards, cost-effectiveness, specialized accreditation, and credentialing.

My first point was that those who administer educational systems need to be proactive agents seeking to discern and maintain quality in their institution. Issues about quality and excellence deserve to be organic to the educational process. However, we shall be living in a world that by and large values us less than we value ourselves. This means that our communication strategy for justifying our quality must be as clear and as objective as we can make it. Our institutional evaluations need to be for third-party reviews. Our strategy should be to seek and expect ongoing surveillance and review by social vigilantes. Our attending to gate keeping at our own institutions needs to be a constant internal process that does not wait for an external agency to provoke it. Whatever excellence we believe we have within our schools must be communicable and convincing to persons and agencies outside our institutions.

At the same time, we must remain in charge of our agenda. We can no longer assume that the purposes of our institutions are self-evident and widely supported. We must be sure that we are understood, believed in, and supported. Our first outward task is to articulate who we are and how we justify our existence. A large amount of this task falls to the administrators who symbolize their school. Public relations is essential to the authenticating process. It has little to do with statistics, measures, and institutional research. It has much to do with effective communication of the mission of the school to the broader public, including special-interest groups. Accountability begins with getting our story across convincingly. This includes finding ways to include a broader segment of the public in our institutional services.

Our second task is to obtain and maintain general institutional recognition in the broader society. I take this to be the principle function of regional accreditation, and I believe that this sourcebook comes down in support of regional accreditation, warts and all. Although some states have attempted to provide a similar function through recognition or approval rituals, having states provide this basic validation of educational institutions has a number of serious problems. One is that public higher education is already governed by the states, so that state monitoring of schools encourages state parochialism and domination of the private sector by the public sector. Another way to make this point is to say that state agencies tend to want to regulate education, while regional accreditation wants to evaluate educational institutions. The role that the Council on Postsecondary Accreditation (COPA) will play in guaranteeing that general institutional endorsement is maintained fairly throughout the country remains to be seen. In any case, some basic ongoing validation of our institutions is necessary to their social recognition.

Our third task is to pursue and maintain specialized and professional recognition, which often relates to the credentialing and licensing of graduates. This sourcebook demonstrates that this trend is already out of hand. The number of groups that want to enforce specialized accreditation has grown remarkably during the past twenty years, and we are rapidly becoming a credentialing society. I believe that most of these specialized accrediting groups have at least as much self-interest as they have interest in quality control and consumer protection, and therefore I remain wary of them. These accrediting groups dictate the qualifications that people whom educational institutions hire should have, what constitutes an acceptable curriculum, and what graduates have to do in order to obtain a license. While we must produce graduates who have competence for professional practice, the meaning of quality in our educational systems is fundamentally more our business than it is the business of accrediting agencies. Recently, a proposal (Brodie and Heaney, 1978) was made to create an interprofessional accrediting council that would require specialized accrediting groups to work together within agreed upon procedures and standards.

Our biggest failing seems to be with student outcomes. Much of the material in this sourcebook suggests that faculty and administrators spend far too much time justifying teaching, research, and institutional management and that we spend far too little time fostering self-responsible learning and evaluation of learning. It is no secret that graduate education dominates the compartmentalization of knowledge, that these compartments have become educational units in undergraduate schools, and that majors govern the undergraduate curriculum. For the baccalaureate degree, the quality emphasis is on making the major work, and the mobility required by students transferring from school to school helps to sustain the existence of major departments with roughly the same course offerings as a national happening.

Reference

Brodie, D. C., and Heaney, R. P. "Need for Reform in Health Professions Accrediting." *Science,* 1978, *201,* 589-593.

Frederic M. Hudson is president of the Fielding Institute, Santa Barbara, California.

Index

A

Accreditation: and assessment of quality, 9, 12; associations of, 3, 10–11; COPA as coordinating body for, 12; effective use of, 26–27; and evolution of standards, 14–15; during expansion years, 17–18; and federal involvement, 15–18; national bodies of, 16–17; origins and development of, 12–19; process of, 10; and quality of education, 19–26, 35–36; regional bodies of, 12–13, 16; during retrenchment, 18–19; specialized, 13, 17; and testing, 45, 77–78; types of, 10
Adelman, C., 39–54, 85–87
American Association of Bible Colleges, 10, 17
American Association of University Women, 13
American Council on Education, 2, 6, 57, 67
American Medical Association, 13, 78
American Osteopathic Association, 13
Association of American Law Schools, 13
Association of American Universities, 13, 14
Association of American University Professors, 74
Association of Colleges and Secondary Schools of the Southern Association, 12
Association of Independent Colleges and Schools, 10
Astin, A. W., 5, 6, 30, 37, 44, 50, 53, 57, 61, 67

B

Barak, R. J., 33, 37
Baxter, G., 79
Becker, G., 45, 53
Berdahl, R. O., 33, 37
Blackburn, R., 46, 53
Blake, H., 41, 53
Bonham, G. N., 2, 3, 5, 6
Bougle, C., 77, 79

Bowen, H. R., 45, 53, 61, 67
Brodie, D. C., 96, 97
Bungum, J. L., 59, 67

C

California Postsecondary Education Commission, 33, 37
Carnegie Foundation, 13
Carnegie Foundation for the Advancement of Teaching, 15, 27
Committee on Allied Health Education and Accreditation, 17
Computer-assisted instruction (CAI), 41
Conference Board of the Mathematical Sciences, 56
Council on Postsecondary Accreditation, 12, 13, 17, 96
Creager, J. A., 53
Curriculum: Faculty effect on, 58–59; influence of textbooks on, 59–60; quality of, 88–89; students effect on, 56–58

E

Education Commission of the States, 32
Educational Testing Service, 42, 62, 67
Eliot, C. W., 72
Enarson, H. L., 2, 3, 5, 6, 30, 37
Ethics. *See* Standards of higher education, and institutional ethics

F

Faculty. *See* Standards of higher education, and faculty performance
Federation of Regional Accrediting Commissions of Higher Education, 11
Feldman, K. A., 61, 67
Flexner, A., 74, 79
Finn, C. E., 3, 6

G

Gardner, D. P., 56, 67
Glenny, L. A., 31, 37

G.I. Bill. *See* Servicemen's Opportunity Act
Goldberg, E. D., 37
Graduate Management Admissions Test, 43
Graduate Record Examination (GRE), 42, 50, 62-64, 78, 85
Green, K. C., 37

H

Haggerty, M. E., 14, 28
Hamlett, B. D., 29-37
Heaney, R. P., 96, 97
Hegarty, T. J., 81-92
Hemond, M. K., 67
Higher Education Act of 1965, 16, 18, 32
Hofstadter, R., 74, 79
Hudson, F. M., 93-97
Hutchinson, T. W., 78, 79
Hyde, W., 46, 53
Hyman, J., 42, 53

K

Kerr, C., 3, 6
King, M. R., 53
Kirkwood, R., 3, 5, 6

L

Lawrence, J. K., 37
Learning: changes in, 60-61; and communication, 47-48; course-based assessment of, 65; and degree programs, 46; grades as indicators of, 64; standards of, 52-53; and test performance, 45, 62-63
Leone, A. O., 37
London, H., 46, 53, 75, 79
Lowell, A. L., 72, 79

M

Marcus, L. K., 33, 37
Mauksch, H., 50, 53
Mazzuca, L., 48, 53
Melchiori, G. S., 33, 37
Middle States Association of Colleges and Schools, 12, 14
Middle States Commission on Higher Education, 16

Millard, R. C., 32, 37
Millard, R. M., 9-28, 83-84, 94
Morey, A. I., 35, 37
Morison, S. E., 72, 79

N

National Academy of Sciences, 24, 28
National Assessment of Educational Progress, 42
National Association of Trade and Technical Schools, 10
National Commission on Accrediting, 11, 17
National Commission on Excellence in Education, 1, 6, 39, 77, 86, 92
National Commission on Higher Education Issues, 1, 2
National Commission of Regional Accrediting Agencies, 11
National Council for the Accreditation of Teacher Education, 35
National Home Study Council, 10, 16
National Institute of Education, 86
New England Association of Colleges and Secondary Schools, 12
Newcomb, F. M., 51, 67
Newman, J. H., 78, 79
North Central Association of Colleges and Secondary Schools, 12, 14, 30
Northwest Association of Schools and Colleges, 12

O

O'Neill, J. P., 69-79, 86, 89-90

P

Palola, E. G., 37
Panos, R. J., 53
Peterson, P. L., 60, 67

Q

Quality of higher education: and accreditation, 3, 9; administrators' role in, 81-83, 93-97; decline of, 1-2; definitions of, 5, 20-22, 30; evaluation of, 4, 6; improvement of, 3; indexes of, 24-25; and institutional failure, 69-74; and institutional integrity, 91-92; and institutional program quality, 23,

83-84; role of statewide agencies in, 31-33, 36-37, 84-85; state concerns for, 29-30; and state program review, 33-35; and student accomplishment, 22-23, 65-66

R

Rashdall, H., 73, 79
Reed, J., 53
Richardson, G. T., 53, 67

S

Scholastic Aptitude Test (SAT), 42, 44, 86
Servicemen's Opportunity Act, 15. *See also* G.I. Bill
Shedd, C., 76, 79
Smallwood, M. C., 72, 79
Smith, A., 78
Smith, W., 74, 79
Snow, R. E., 60, 67
Society of American Foresters, 13
Solman, L. C., 5, 6
Standards of higher education: and accrediting associations, 14-15, 26; content of, 41-42; and the curriculum, 46-47; definitions of, 20; and faculty performance, 74-76, 86-87; and interinstitutional cooperation, 48-49; and institutional ethics, 51-52; and the market model, 44-45; nature of, 25-26; and the preparation of faculty, 49-50; and relationship to accreditation, 52-53, 76-77; and role of examinations, 77-78, 85-86; and student performance, 42-44
State Higher Education Executive Officers, 32
Stevens, J., 29-37
Students. *See* Curriculum, student effects on; Standards of higher education, and student performance

T

Tests. *See* Learning, and test performance
Trow, M., 40, 51, 54

U

Ullman, A. D., 52, 54

V

Veysey, L., 58, 67

W

Warren, J. R., 1-7, 55-67, 74, 82, 83, 88-89
Weisz, G., 53
Western Association of Schools and Colleges, 35
Western College Association, 12
Wright, C., 53

Z

Zook, G. F., 14, 28

Ministry of Education, Ontario
Information Services & Resources Unit,
13th Floor, Mowat Block, Queen's Park,
Toronto   M7A 1L2